REALISM

Coming to prominence with the nineteenth-century novel, literary realism has traditionally been associated with an insistence that art cannot turn away from the harsher, more sordid aspects of human existence. However, the fluid nature of the related concepts of 'reality' and 'the real' have led to realism becoming one of the most widely debated terms to be covered in this series.

Realism offers an accessible account of literary realism as a distinctive mode of writing, setting out the defining attributes of the genre and exploring the critical debates surrounding it, illustrated throughout with examples taken from a wide variety of prose fiction. The book covers the historical development and artistic achievements of literary realism and presents a lucid argument for its continuing status as an innovative and challenging tradition of writing, with rigorous exploration of the radical critique brought to bear on realist forms of representation during the twentieth century from the perspectives of modernism, poststructuralism and postmodernism.

This comprehensive guide is essential reading for any student of literature, and will prove indispensable for those with a particular interest in the realist novel.

Pam Morris is Professor of Modern Critical Studies at Liverpool John Moores University and has written extensively on nineteenth-century literature and culture. She is the editor of *The Bakhtin Reader* (1994) and author of *Literature and Feminism* (1993) and *Imagining Inclusive Society in Nineteenth-Century Novels: The Code of Sincerity in the Public Sphere* (2004).

THE NEW CRITICAL IDIOM

SERIES EDITOR: JOHN DRAKAKIS, UNIVERSITY OF STIRLING

The New Critical Idiom is an invaluable series of introductory guides to today's critical terminology. Each book:

- provides a handy, explanatory guide to the use (and abuse) of the term
- offers an original and distinctive overview by a leading literary and cultural critic
- relates the term to the larger field of cultural representation

With a strong emphasis on clarity, lively debate and the widest possible breadth of examples, *The New Critical Idiom* is an indispensable approach to key topics in literary studies.

Also available in this series:

REALISM

Pam Morris

Routledge
Taylor & Francis Group

LONDON AND NEW YORK

First published 2003
by Routledge
2 Park Square, Milton Park, Abingdon, Oxon OX14 4RN

Simultaneously published in the USA and Canada
by Routledge
270 Madison Avenue, New York, NY 10016

Routledge is an imprint of the Taylor & Francis Group,
an informa business

Reprinted 2005, 2009

Typeset in Garamond by Taylor & Francis Books Ltd
Printed and bound in Great Britain by the MPG Books Group

British Library Cataloguing in Publication Data
A catalogue record for this book is available from the British Library

Library of Congress Cataloging-in-Publication Data
Morris, P, 1940–
Realism/Pam Morris.
p. cm. – (New critical idiom)
Includes bibliographical references (p.) and index.
1. European literature – 19th century – History and criticism. 2.
Realism in literature. I. Title. II. Series.
PN761.M625 2003
809'.912'09409034–dc21   2002156322

ISBN 978–0–415–22938–8 (hbk)
ISBN 978–0–415–22939–5 (pbk)

For Vicky

CONTENTS

PART III
LITERARY REALISM AS FORMAL ART

PART IV
REALISM AND KNOWLEDGE: A UTOPIAN PROJECT?

SERIES EDITOR'S PREFACE

The New Critical Idiom is a series of introductory books which seeks to extend the lexicon of literary terms, in order to address the radical changes which have taken place in the study of literature during the last decades of the twentieth century. The aim is to provide clear, well-illustrated accounts of the full range of terminology currently in use, and to evolve histories of its changing usage.

The current state of the discipline of literary studies is one where there is considerable debate concerning basic questions of terminology. This involves, among other things, the boundaries which distinguish the literary from the non-literary; the position of literature within the larger sphere of culture; the relationship between literatures of different cultures; and questions concerning the relation of literary to other cultural forms within the context of interdisciplinary studies.

It is clear that the field of literary criticism and theory is a dynamic and heterogeneous one. The present need is for individual volumes on terms which combine clarity of exposition with an adventurousness of perspective and a breadth of application. Each volume will contain as part of its apparatus some indication of the direction in which the definition of particular terms is likely to move, as well as expanding the disciplinary boundaries within which some of these terms have been traditionally contained. This will involve some re-situation of terms within the larger field of cultural representation, and will introduce examples from the area of film and the modern media in addition to examples from a variety of literary texts.

ACKNOWLEDGEMENTS

I would like to thank John Drakakis and Liz Thompson for their generous and supportive editorial concern throughout the writing of this book.

INTRODUCTION
What is Realism?

'John MacNaughton was nothing if not a realist.' Imagine you have just opened the first page of a novel in a book shop. What expectations about the character will have been raised by the final word of the sentence? Would you be inclined to put the book back on the shelf or take it to the till? Very sensibly, you would probably read a bit more, but let us assume you are an impulse buyer. In which case, you may have thought: 'Now, here is a character I can fully sympathise with as pursuing a clear-sighted, unromantic approach to life. Whatever problems the fictional John McNaughton meets in the course of the story I shall enjoy the way he responds rationally and practically, overcoming difficulties by an accurate evaluation of all the facts of the situation that avoids self-indulgent whimsy and sentimentality.' On the other hand, you might have rejected the book as featuring a protagonist who will lack vision and high idealism; you may feel that literature must aspire to truths and values beyond the everyday mundane. The approach to life indicated by the first response is most briskly encapsulated in the advice to 'Get real!' and perhaps its most uncompromising fictional advocate is Mr Gradgrind, in Charles Dickens's *Hard Times*, who insists: 'Now what I want is, Facts. Teach these boys and girls nothing but Facts. Facts alone are wanted in life' ([1854] 1989: 1). To which, a non-fictional Victorian contemporary of Gradgrind might well have responded severely, 'It is a fact, sir, that man has a material body, but the only true reality that concerns man is his spiritual soul.'

What is demonstrated here is the slippery nature of the related terms realist and realism and the difficulties involved in defining them in any precise and unambiguous way. In the first place, the terms realism and realist inhabit both the realm of everyday usage and the more specialist aesthetic realm of literary and artistic usage. As we can see above, in ordinary speech situations there is frequent traffic between these two realms. Inevitably our judgements about fictional characters and novels are generally influenced by our attitudes to non-fictional reality. It is impossible to draw absolute boundaries separating the meaning and values of the terms as they are normally used from their evaluative meaning as used in critical discourse. Related to this is the entanglement of realist and realism with a series of other words equally resistant to clear-cut definition: factuality, truth, reality, realistic and real. Sometimes these words are taken to have roughly the same meaning as realist but equally they are sometimes used to stake out the opposite. This points to the third area of problem: the term realism almost always involves both claims about the nature of reality and an evaluative attitude towards it. It is, thus, a term that is frequently invoked in making fundamental ethical and political claims or priorities, based upon perceptions of what is 'true' or 'real'. As such, the usage is often contentious and polemical.

In *Humanism* (1997), Tony Davies describes 'realism' as one of those words 'whose range of possible meanings runs from the pedantically exact to the cosmically vague' (p.3). I cannot offer any exact definition but I will attempt to avoid both undue vagueness and cosmic proportions as to what is considered under the term. Because of its association with claims about reality, the concept of 'realism' participates in scientific and philosophical debates. The visual arts, theatre and film have all developed quite distinctive traditions of realism as a representational form. Due to limitations of space, I shall restrict my consideration primarily to literary realism only drawing upon philosophical and scientific issues where these have direct relevance to writerly forms. I shall also deal pre-eminently with the novel genre since it is within prose fiction that realism as an art form has been most fully developed.

The inherently oppositional nature of the word 'realism' is brought out in one of the definitions offered in the Oxford English Dictionary (OED) as 'any view or system contrasted with idealism'. Idealism, as a system of thought that subordinates sensory perceptions of the world to intellectual or spiritual knowledge, is often also opposed to the term 'materialism', which the OED defines as the doctrine that nothing exists but matter, the stuff that constitutes the physical universe. This brings us back again to the central question of what constitutes reality. The debate over this goes back certainly as far as the ancient world but the issue between idealism and materialism came especially to the fore during the eighteenth and nineteenth centuries with the rise of the empirical sciences like botany, anatomy and geology. For the first time the authority of metaphysical and divine truth came under challenge from a secular form of knowledge that claimed to reveal the truth of the material physical world. By and large, the development of the realist novel coincided with and aligned itself to the modern secular materialist understanding of reality. Realist plots and characters are constructed in accordance with secular empirical rules. Events and people in the story are explicable in terms of natural causation without resort to the supernatural or divine intervention. Whereas idealism is grounded upon a view of Truth as universal and timeless, **empiricism** finds its truths in the **particular** and specific. Yet this does not prevent the sympathetic treatment of idealism or of a character's religious beliefs within the narrative. The struggle of an idealist against the hampering materiality of the social world is a structuring device of a great many realist novels. In fact, one could argue that realist forms have given expression to some of the most powerful representations of spiritual conviction and commitment. The character Levin in Leo Tolstoy's (1928–1910) *Anna Karenina* (1875–7), for example, discovers meaning in life only through a religious revelation.

Yet undeniably realism as a literary form has been associated with an insistence that art cannot turn away from the more sordid and harsh aspects of human existence. The stuff of realism is not selected for its dignity and nobility. More positively, realism participates in the democratic impulse of modernity. As a genre, it has reached out to a much wider social range, in terms both of readership and of characters represented, than earlier more élite forms of literature. In particular, realism, as a form uninfluenced by classical conventions, has been developed by women writers and women readers from its beginnings. Thus, as an upstart literary form, the novel lacked the cultural capital or prestige of traditional forms like poetry and drama. Novels also were the first literary products to discover a mass market and they made some of their writers a great deal of money. For all of these reasons novels were open to attack as materialist in a pejorative sense by those who felt a need to defend a more spiritual expression of human existence. So, for example, the poet Algernon Charles Swinburne (1837–1909) drew a distinction between 'prosaic realism' and 'poetic reality'. In tracing the debates that have developed around realism as a literary form, it becomes apparent that issues about its relationship to the non-fictional or non-textual world are frequently influenced by fears about mass culture. Novels were perhaps the first popular form to be accused of 'dumbing down'.

There is one distinction between realist writing and actual everyday reality beyond the text that must be quite categorically insisted upon: realist novels *never* give us life or a slice of life nor do they reflect reality. In the first place, literary realism is a representational form and a representation can never be identical with that which it represents. In the second place, words function completely differently from mirrors. If you think for a moment about a mirror reflecting a room and compare it to a detailed written description of the room, then reversal of images aside, it is obvious that no writing can encompass every tiny visual detail as a mirror faithfully does. Writing has to select and order, something has to come first, and that selection and ordering will always, in some way, entail the values and perspective of the describer. Furthermore, no matter how convincing the prose is in its rendering of social reality, even the most realist of texts deploys writerly conventions that have no equivalent in experiential reality: use of punctuation, denotations like 'he said'. Indeed, if we accept too quickly or unquestioningly the assumption that realist texts copy reality we tend to overlook a long, impressive tradition of artistic development during which writers struggled and experimented with the artistic means to convey a verbal sense of what it is like to live an embodied existence in the world. This history of experimental prose fiction is one of great artistic achievement. Realism is a technically demanding medium. Part III of this book will explore some of the complex and impressive formal devices that constitute the art form of realism as a genre.

The OED gets nearest to the sense of realism as a representational form in its definition: 'close resemblance to what is real; fidelity of representation, the rendering of precise details of the real thing or scene.' Closely associated with this meaning are the two terms '**mimesis**' and '**verisimilitude**' that often crop up in discussions of realism as an art form. Mimesis is a term that derives from classical Greek drama where it referred to the actors' direct imitation of words and actions. This is perhaps the most exact form of correspondence or fidelity between representation and actuality. As it developed as a critical term, the meaning of mimesis has gradually widened to encompass the general idea of close artistic imitation of social reality, although it is occasionally restricted in use to refer only to those textual passages in which characters appear to speak and act for themselves in contradistinction to narrative commentary. I shall use mimesis in the former wider sense. 'Verisimilitude' is defined as 'the appearance of being true or real; likeness or resemblance to truth, reality or fact'.

The problem with definitions of realism and related terms that use phrases like 'fidelity of representation' or 'rendering of precise details' is that they tend to be associated with notions of truth as verifiability. There is a popular and somewhat paradoxical assumption that realist fiction is to be judged according to how faithfully it corresponds to things and events in the real-world. The more exact the correspondence, the more a one-to-one concordance can be recognised between words and world, the more the realist writer is to be praised as having achieved her or his aim. Realist novels developed as a popular form during the nineteenth century alongside the other quickly popularised representational practice of photography. This coincidence may well have encouraged a pictorial or photographic model of truth as correspondence. We have probably all pointed a camera at a scene or person and been pleased at the likeness reproduced. Yet, as I stressed above there can be no simple identification of verbal with visual representations and both are equally distinct from the actuality they convey. Practised seriously, photography and realist fiction are distinctive art forms that carefully select, organise and structure their representations of the world. The selection and arrangement of verbal and visual codes or languages are governed by very different rules. In fact, as we shall see in Part II, there is little evidence to suggest that the major realist writers of the nineteenth century ever saw their goal in terms of a one-to-one correspondence with a non-verbal reality. Nevertheless, it was this kind of perception of realism's aims as accurate reportage or 'reflection' that aroused the criticism of idealists who invoked truths that lay beyond the surface appearance of things. During the latter part of the twentieth century, however, realism has suffered a far more radical attack upon its artistic integrity. Realist writing has been caught up in a much larger controversy which has put in question the whole tradition of knowledge and truth as it developed from the eighteenth through to the twentieth century. Within this critique, it is the capacity of novels to communicate any truths at all about human existence in the real-world beyond the text that comes under fire.

From this sceptical, anti-realist framework it is sometimes suggested that the term 'realism' should be confined to the specific period of the nineteenth century when novelists like Honoré de Balzac (1799–1850) wrote within a historical context in which the possibility of observational truth about the world was unquestioned. This was certainly the period when realism, especially in France, was most consciously avowed and debated as an artistic form and Part II gives an account of the achievements of realist writers during those innovative decades. However, realism as artistic practice has much wider historical scope than the nineteenth century: aspects that we want to call realist can be found in Chaucer's writing and in even earlier classical literature while today artistically innovative realist novels are still being produced. Even in writing that seems to adopt a mode of expression very far from realist representation, there are frequently passages that move into realist style. For this reason, although a water-tight definition of realism is impossible we continue to need the term within the discourse of literary criticism. As a starting point I shall define literary realism as any writing that is based upon an implicit or explicit assumption that it is possible to communicate about a reality beyond the writing. I shall attempt to define and support that claim most fully in the final chapter. In Part I, I outline the historical development of the radical twentieth-century critique of the grounds of knowledge, or **epistemology**, for realism and explore the political and social controversies that are involved in such scepticism.

I

REALISM VERSUS EXPERIMENTALISM?

1

REALISM AND MODERNISM

THE PRACTICE OF LITERARY REALISM

Realism, I have suggested, is a notoriously tricky term to define. Even when limited to the realm of literary writing it has an aesthetic and a cognitive dimension neither of which can be wholly separated one from the other. Aesthetically, realism refers to certain modes and conventions of verbal and visual representation that can occur at any historical time. Yet realism is associated particularly with the secular and rational forms of knowledge that constitute the tradition of the **Enlightenment**, stemming from the growth of scientific understanding in the eighteenth century. Underpinning Enlightenment thought is an optimistic belief that human beings can adequately reproduce, by means of verbal and visual representations, both the **objective** world that is exterior to them and their own **subjective** responses to that exteriority. Such representations, verbal and visual, are assumed to be mutually recognisable by fellow human beings and form the basis of knowledge about the physical and social worlds. The values of accuracy, adequacy and truth are fundamental to this empirical view of knowledge and its representational form: realism. It follows from this that literary modes of writing that can be recognised as realist are those that, broadly speaking, present themselves as corresponding to the world as it is, using language predominantly as a means of communication rather than verbal display, and offering rational, secular explanations for all the happenings of the world so represented. Two central theses drive the argument I shall develop throughout this book: firstly, questions of knowledge and **relative truth** are inseparable from an understanding of realism as a representational form and secondly, our ability to communicate reasonably accurately with each other about the world and ourselves is what makes human community possible. Perhaps not surprisingly, the literary genre most closely associated with realism is the novel, which developed during the eighteenth century alongside Enlightenment thought and alongside more generally that most secular mode of human existence: capitalism. For this reason, aesthetic evaluations of realism are frequently informed by or entangled with views on the development of the Enlightenment, the expansion of capitalist production and the emergence of a modern mass culture.

But before moving on to questions of how literary realism has been evaluated, it will be useful to look at a piece of realist prose to see how far it conforms to the **paradigm** I have set out above. George Eliot (1819–80) is usually regarded as one of the most accomplished of English nineteenth-century realist novelists. Here is the opening of her final novel, *Daniel Deronda* (1874–6):

> Was she beautiful or not beautiful? And what was the secret of form or expression which gave the dynamic quality to her glance? Was the good or the evil genius dominant in those beams? Probably the evil; else why was the effect of unrest rather than undisturbed charm? Why was the wish to look again felt as coercion and not as a longing in which the whole being consents?
>
> She who raised these questions in Daniel Deronda's mind was occupied in gambling: not in the open air under a southern sky, tossing coppers on a ruined wall, with rags about her limbs; but in one of those splendid resorts which the enlightenment of ages has prepared for the same species of pleasure at a heavy cost of gilt mouldings, dark-toned colour and chubby nudities, all correspondingly heavy – forming a suitable condenser for human breath belonging, in great part, to the highest fashion, and not easily procurable to be breathed in elsewhere in the like proportion, at least by persons of little fashion.

It was near four o'clock on a September day, so that the atmosphere was well-brewed to a visible haze. There was deep stillness, broken only by a light rattle, a light chink, a small sweeping sound, and an occasional monotone in French, such as might be expected to issue from an ingeniously constructed automaton. Round two long tables were gathered two serried crowds of human beings, all save one having their faces and attention bent on the table. The one exception was a melancholy little boy, with his knees and calves simply in their natural clothing of epidermis, but for the rest of his person in a fancy dress. He alone had his face turned towards the doorway, and fixing on it the blank gaze of a bedizened child stationed as a masquerading advertisement on the platform of an itinerant show, stood close behind a lady deeply engaged at the roulette-table.

(Eliot [1874–6] 1988: 3–4)

It seems obvious that what is being foregrounded here is the human capacity to perceive an external reality and thereby come to know it. The questions that construct the first paragraph arise in the mind of Deronda as he observes an attractive woman engaged in gambling. Accustomed novel readers will expect their own uncertainty as well as Deronda's to be transformed into firm knowledge by the end of the story. In this, Eliot's beginning of *Daniel Deronda* only makes explicit what is implicit in the opening pages of most realist fictions: questions are raised about characters and situations which will be resolved by fuller knowledge gained during the course of the narrative. In this respect, the reader's epistemological progress through novels imitates the way we acquire empirical knowledge of the actual social and physical worlds by means of observation of factual details, behaviour and events. Deronda's questions indicate his lack of present knowledge about Gwendolin Harleth, the heroine, but the language of his speculations surely suggests a confident reliance upon an existing structure of evaluative meaning which will provide a shaping framework for whatever factual details he obtains about the woman he observes. 'Was she beautiful or not beautiful?...Was the good or evil genius dominant in those beams?' There seems little suggestion in these either/or formulations that there may be qualities of personality that are simply unknowable or beyond aesthetic and moral recognition and categorisation. The subsequent characterisation of Gwendolin also conforms to the positive epistemology as expansion of knowledge that underlies realist writing. The story traces Gwendolin's painful emotional and rational process towards self-awareness and moral certainty and in so doing constitutes for the reader that sense of a complex, intimately known, individual psychology that is one of the achievements of nineteenth-century fiction.

If we move on to the tone and language of the **omniscient narrator** (see **narrator**) in the subsequent paragraphs, it is clear that they rest upon a confident sense that understanding of the world can be truthfully reproduced and communicated in verbal form. The narrator's capacious knowledge of gambling allows open air penny-tossing to be brought into telling conjunction with the play at fashionable resorts. The perspective unites knowledgeable generalisation ('in one of those splendid resorts which the enlightenment of ages has prepared for the same species of pleasure') with empirical specificity ('It was near four o'clock on a September day, so that the atmosphere was well-brewed to a visible haze'). In the paragraph following the extract given above, the writing traces the movement from empirical observation of the external world to inductive knowledge of its underlying economic energies. The narrator notes that the activity of gambling brings together an assortment of nationalities and social classes not usually seen in such proximity to each other. Sitting close by a countess is a sleekly respectable London tradesman: 'Not his the gambler's passion that nullifies appetite, but a well-fed leisure, which in the intervals of winning money in business and spending it showily, sees no better resources than winning money in play and spending it yet more showily' (Eliot [1874–6] 1988: 4). The novel's opening image of gambling thus crystallises a historical insight into the development of speculative forms of capitalism in the second half of the nineteenth-century. As the quotation above suggests, speculative finance was intimately associated with the expansion of consumerism.

During the twentieth century, realist writing such as this became the focus of critical attack during two separate but related periods which can be thought of as the moment of **modernism** and the moment of **postmodernism**. The exact duration of both modernism and postmodernism is still a matter of historical and critical debate, as is the relationship between them. (For a succinct account of this debate see Brooker 1992: 1–29.) Some commentators argue for a continuity from modernism into postmodernism and some insist upon a distinct aesthetic and epistemological break. Our only concern with this complex history is how it impinges upon the practice and understanding of realist writing. For this purpose it makes sense to recognise modernist experimentation with traditional narrative form as beginning with writers like Joseph Conrad (1857–1924) in the last years of the nineteenth century and continuing into the 1920s and 1930s with the publication of James Joyce's *Ulysses* (1922) and *Finnegans Wake* (1939). The earliest references to postmodernism come from American cultural critics in the 1950s and the term has developed as a means of theorising the geographical and historical world of late capitalism. (Jameson 1998 contains essays exploring some of the main issues of American postmodernism; see especially 'Theories of the Postmodern', 21–32. Brooker 1992 also offers key writing on postmodernism and excellent bibliographies for further reading.) A third term, 'poststructuralism', is also closely interwoven with this complex intellectual history. As a theoretical perspective, poststructuralism has offered both a critical approach to modernist and postmodernist forms of art and has itself profoundly influenced the way artists understand their role. By and large, a French-influenced American perspective on postmodernism has tended to dominate critical thinking in Britain since the 1980s as opposed to a somewhat differently inflected German theoretical understanding. What is most relevant for us at this point is that all three of these 'isms', modernism, postmodernism and poststructuralism, have tended to define themselves against their own versions of realism and in so doing have produced a many-faceted critique of realist forms of writing that has become the dominant critical orthodoxy. So it makes sense to start by understanding the development of this rather negative view of realism that most readers are likely to encounter. I will start chronologically in this chapter with the relationship of modernism to realism and in the following chapter turn to postmodernism.

THE MODERNIST CRITIQUE OF REALISM

Here, by way of comparison with Eliot's realist writing, is the opening passage of *Mrs Dalloway*, a modernist novel written by Virginia Woolf (1882–1941) in 1925.

> Mrs Dalloway said she would buy the flowers herself.
>
> For Lucy had her work cut out for her. The doors would be taken off their hinges; Rumpelmayer's men were coming. And then, thought Clarissa Dalloway, what a morning – fresh as if issued to children on a beach.
>
> What a lark! What a plunge! For so it had always seemed to her when, with a little squeak of the hinges, which she could hear now, she had burst open the French windows at Bourton into the open air. How fresh, how calm, stiller than this of course, the air was in the early morning; like the flap of a wave; the kiss of a wave; chill and sharp and yet (for a girl of eighteen as she then was) solemn, feeling as she did, standing there at the open window, that something awful was about to happen; looking at the flowers, at the trees with the smoke winding off them and the rooks rising, falling: standing and looking until Peter Walsh said, 'Musing among the vegetables?' – was that it? – 'I prefer men to cauliflowers' – was that it? He must have said it at breakfast one morning when she had gone out onto the ter-race – Peter Walsh. He would be back from India one of these days, June or July, she forgot which, for his letters were awfully dull; it was his sayings one remembered; his eyes, his pocket-knife, his smile, his grumpiness and, when millions of things had utterly vanished – how strange it was! – a few sayings like this about cabbages.
>
> (Woolf [1925] 1992: 3)

Superficially these first paragraphs have much in common with the opening of *Daniel Deronda*. Both passages convey a sense of entering immediately into the midst of things, both focus upon a central female character and both contain the voice of a third person narrator. Yet there is surely a vast difference in the assumptions about knowledge that underlie each piece of writing. Despite the use of an impersonal narra-tive voice, no objective perspective is offered the reader of *Mrs Dalloway* from which to understand and evaluate the characters referred to or the social world evoked. The **focalisation**, or narrative perspective, remains almost entirely within the subjective consciousness of Clarissa Dalloway; it is her way of knowing things that the writing aims to convey. Yet 'knowledge' in any traditional sense is hardly the appropriate word for the subjective continuum of personal thoughts, memories, sensory responses, speculations and emotions that constitutes the second paragraph. The 'character', Clarissa Dalloway, thus produced is too fluid, multiple, changing, and amorphous to become a fully comprehended object of the reader's knowledge. Although the past is evoked, there is no sense of progressive, rational self-development over time: of a moral growth of awareness and enlightenment as the adult learns from earlier errors and misunderstanding. In Clarissa's consciousness the past remains an active force flowing into each current moment but intellectual understanding seems much less important than the sharp recall of physical sensation inseparably bound to an emotion still felt freshly on the pulses. This passage is typical of the whole novel in which the 'plot' is encompassed in a single day and resolves no mysteries, leaves the future of the lives presented in the story as uncertain as at the beginning, and refuses the reader any objective knowledge of the main protagonists that could form the basis of moral or epistemological evaluation. Put in technical terms the novel refuses **closure**: nothing and no-one is summed up in the writing as a coherent truth that can be known. As a final point we should notice the very different way in which Woolf uses language to that of Eliot. Rather than understanding words primarily as a means of accurate communication transmission, Woolf foregrounds their creative capacity. Mrs Dalloway's thought process is not explained rationally to the reader in the way the narrator of *Daniel Deronda* explains the gambling psychology of the wealthy London tradesman, rather, in *Mrs Dalloway*, the rhythm and sound of words are utilised to directly suggest something of the actual texture and flow of inner feeling. A few sayings about cabbages constitutes Peter Walsh in his immediacy for Clarissa Dalloway in a way that factual details about him cannot.

Virginia Woolf (1882–1941) was part of the early twentieth-century avant-garde movement of modernist writers for whom realist narratives had come to seem stylistically cumbersome, over-concerned with detailed description of things, their plots determined by narrow middle-class morality, and exuding a naive and philistine confidence that objective truth about reality entailed only accurate reportage of sufficient material details. These criticisms are forcefully expressed in Woolf's well-known essay, 'Mr Bennett and Mrs Brown' (1924) in which she attacks the realist tradition of novel writing as it was currently being practised by a somewhat earlier generation of writers like Arnold Bennett (1867–1931). Bennett was so concerned to provide a documentary inventory of social aspects about his fictional characters, Woolf claims, that the essence of personality escaped him (Woolf [1924] 1967: I. 319–37). In another essay on 'Modern Fiction' (1925) she argues that reality as actually experienced by each of us is composed of 'a myriad impressions – trivial, fantastic, evanescent, or engraved with the sharpness of steel.' She asks 'Is it not the task of the novelist to convey this varying, this unknown and uncircumscribed spirit, whatever aberration or complexity it may display, with as little mixture of the alien and external as possible?' (Woolf [1925] 1972: II. 106). The opposition Woolf sets up in these essays between a realist absorption in the surface materiality of things, on the one hand, and an 'uncircumscribed spirit' as artistic consciousness of subjective reality on the other, suggests that in part, at least, modernist writers were reacting against the increasing consumerism and mass production of their culture. One element within modernism is a somewhat fastidious repulsion at what they felt was the philistine materialism of much of middle-class life and tastes. As popular literature and other forms of art became objects of mass production and consumption, serious writers were challenged to re-assert the claims of art for art's sake in a way that earlier writers like Charles Dickens and George Eliot, for example, had not been.

There is also a sense in which criticism of realist writing made by modernist writers like Woolf was in large part the invariable revolt of a younger generation against their literary precursors. Yet, importantly, the claims asserted by modernist writers for their own work largely retained the evaluative language of the Enlightenment. Their art was new and often aimed to shock bourgeois complacencies, but their goal remained the pursuit of truth. Woolf quarrelled with Bennett because she believed that the orderly pattern imposed on life by much realist fiction was inaccurate. Joseph Conrad, experimenting with narrative form at the end of the nineteenth century, developed his modernist techniques in the service of literary art – 'defined as a single-minded attempt to render the highest kind of justice to the visible universe, by bringing to light the truth, manifold and one, underlying its every aspect....The artist, then, like the thinker or the scientist, seeks the truth and makes his appeal' (Conrad [1897] 1988: xlvii). In the 1930s, James Joyce explained that his aim in *Ulysses* was to present the hero, Leopold Bloom, as a complete human being, seen from all sides, in all human relationships, an anatomical human body that 'lives in and moves through space and is the home of a full human personality' (quoted in Budgen 1989: 21). Modernist writers wrote out of a troubled sense that 'reality', whether material or psychological, was elusive, complex, multiple and unstable, but they still believed that the aim of their art was to convey knowledge, by some new aesthetic means, of that intangibility. In this sense, their quarrel with realism was predominantly an aesthetic and epistemological one. However, during the 1930s and 1940s, the oppressive dictatorship of Stalin in Russia and the growth of **fascism** in Germany produced a cultural climate in which all public debates, including the contending claims of realism and modernist experimentation, became highly politicised. This polemical conflict, which inevitably veers towards over-simplification, has tended to dominate all subsequent discussion and evaluation of realist representation.

THE FRANKFURT SCHOOL: MODERNISM VERSUS REALISM

The most powerful advocacy for modernist art came from a group of German cultural critics, influenced by **Marxism**, who were associated, during the 1930s, with the Frankfurt Institute for Social Research. Subsequently known collectively as the Frankfurt School, members of this group produced a series of brilliant cultural diagnoses of what they saw as the malaise of contemporary society, symptomatic in the rise of **fascism** and mass consumerism. These diagnostic essays transformed the aesthetic repulsion at increasing materialism expressed by many modernist writers into the intellectual foundation of modern cultural and media studies. Members of the Frankfurt School claimed that the root of modern political and cultural intolerance and repressive moral and social conformity lay in the collaborative relationship that had developed between the Enlightenment and **capitalism**. The fullest account of this, *Dialectic of Enlightenment* (1944), by Theodor Adorno (1903–69) and Max Horkheimer (1895–1973), begins strikingly: 'In the most general sense of progressive thought, the Enlightenment has always aimed at liberating men from fear and establishing their sovereignty. Yet the fully enlightened earth radiates disaster triumphant' (Adorno and Horkheimer [1944] 1997: 3).

According to Adorno and Horkheimer, disaster attends the project of the Enlightenment because knowledge came to be understood as a form of rational **functionalism**. In other words, knowledge was desired only as a means of mastering and making use of the world. Implicit in such a view is a hostility towards any form of mystery. What is unknown becomes a source of fear rather than reverence. Knowledge is a means of human empowerment, Adorno and Horkheimer acknowledge, but 'Men pay for the increase of their power with alienation from that over which they exercise power. Enlightenment behaves towards things as a dictator towards men. He knows them in so far as he can manipulate them' (Adorno and Horkheimer [1944] 1997: 9). The logical result of this functional pursuit of knowledge is ever greater rationalisation and systematisation; the ideal of knowledge and language becomes mathematical certainty. (This ideal was formulated by Bertrand Russell and taken up by logical positivist philosophers. A fuller account of this will be given in Chapter 4.) Thus the Enlightenment lost the capacity for a questioning, **self-reflexive** knowledge that could have produced understanding of its own dangers and limitations. Human beings and objects alike are categorised, regularised and unified into the conforming mass order required by a capitalist mode of production and consumption. 'Through the countless agencies of mass production and its culture,' Adorno and Horkheimer write, 'the conventionalised modes of behaviour are impressed on the individual as the only natural, respectable and rational ones.' (Adorno and Horkheimer [1944] 1997: 28).

It can be argued that realist fiction, mass produced as part of this consumer culture, is complicit with functional rationalism. Popular novels written in a realist mode can function to naturalise a banal view of the world as familiar, morally and socially categorised and predictable. Such stories reproduce the gender, class and racial stereotypes that predominate in society at large; waywardness and unconventionality of any kind are shown, by means of the plot structure, to lead to punishment and failure of some kind, while morally and socially condoned patterns of behaviour are those rewarded by wealth and opportunities in the case of heroes and love and marriage in the case of heroines. The implicit epistemological message of such realist writing is to insist 'this is how it is', this is 'just the way things are and always will be'. Art as a special form of knowledge-seeking gives way to art as diversion from any troubling reality and 'enlightenment becomes wholesale deception of the masses.' (Adorno and Horkheimer [1944] 1997: 42). Adorno and Horkheimer argue that the end product of the Enlightenment has not been an increase in human freedom as promised but, on the contrary, the enclosure of all human existence within a total system that is seamlessly controlled by the culture industry, multinational capitalism and bureaucratic forms of power. As we shall see, throughout the critique of Enlightenment and realism that Part I traces, images of entrapment and enclosure are recurrently applied to both mass culture and realist writing.

Despite the severity of Adorno's and Horkheimer's attack upon the project of Enlightenment, there is a degree of ambiguity in the way the term 'enlightenment' is used in *Dialectic of Enlightenment*. As the title suggests, the aim is not a wholesale rejection of all progressive thought. The real focus of the critique would appear to be what is at times called the bourgeois enlightenment as the pursuit of a dominating functional rationality. This leaves the suggestion, at least, that a positive self-reflexive form of enlightenment could emerge and in so doing produce a critique of the alienating **totalising** system of mass culture. Within this logic it is also arguable that some kinds of realist art can offer a form of knowledge that constitutes just such a **negative critique**. A later member of the Frankfurt School, Jürgen Habermas (1929–), has subsequently advanced a defence of the Enlightenment project and we shall come to his ideas and their implications for a positive understanding of realism in the final chapter.

The only concrete example Adorno offers of this negative kind of knowledge is that achieved by the experimental, avant-garde works of modernist writers like Franz Kafka (1883–1924) and Samuel Beckett (1906–89). 'Art is the negative knowledge of the actual world,' he writes, a knowledge produced by the distancing effect of aesthetic innovation (translated in Taylor 1980: 160). Kafka's prose and Beckett's plays have the effect of 'dismantling appearances' so that 'the inescapability of their work compels the change of attitude which committed works merely demand' (Taylor 1980: 191). By 'committed works' Adorno largely means traditional realist forms of writing and he argues that 'Art does not provide knowledge of reality by reflecting it photographically...but by revealing whatever is veiled by the empirical form assumed by reality' (Taylor 1980: 162). Realist art he argues in an essay on Kafka accepts 'the facade of reality at face-value' whereas in the work of Kafka 'the space-time of 'empirical realism' is exploded through small acts of sabotage, like perspective in contemporary painting' (Adorno [1967] 1983: 261). How vulnerable is George Eliot's realism to such criticism of realist form? If not exactly photographic, the extract from *Daniel Deronda* at the beginning of this chapter certainly aims at a strong effect of verisimilitude in its representation of the chink and sweep of money sounds and the visual appearance of the gaming room, with the rapt attention of the gamblers set against the melancholy, blank gaze of the little boy, incongruous in such a setting. The people assembled are individualised as sharply detailed visual portraits: 'the square, gaunt face, deep-set eyes, grizzled eye-brows, and ill-combed scanty hair' of the English countess contrasted to the London tradesman , 'blond and soft-handed, his sleek hair scrupulously parted behind and before' (Eliot [1874–6] 1988: 4). There are no acts of artistic sabotage here to make us doubt the temporal and spatial certainty of the world represented. Furthermore, Eliot's readiness to categorise her characters morally and socially might be seen as complicit with the systematising impulse of knowledge as mastery that Adorno associates with the Enlightenment. However, in defence of Eliot's realism, we might want to question how far her writing accepts at face-value the façade of social reality; the recognition of gambling as an image of the dynamics of speculative capitalism surely suggests a more complex understanding of the structural and economic forces of her age.

A more damaging charge against realism than that of epistemological complacency is Adorno's claim that the representation of acts of suffering and atrocity in popular art contains 'however remotely, the power to elicit enjoyment out of it' (Taylor 1980: 189). This argument undermines the validity of claims that have been central to the long political tradition of realist writing – that powerful depiction of suffering and injustice can act as a vehicle for social reform and change. It was the force of this belief, that graphic accounts of injustice could shock the public conscience into more progressive attitudes and behaviour, that provided the motive for passionate protest fictions like Harriet Beecher Stowe's (1811–1896) novel *Uncle Tom's Cabin* (1851), for example. It was certainly a belief at the heart of Dickens's writing. Less spectacularly, in terms of *Daniel Deronda*, it raises the question as to whether Eliot's negative view of gambling, highlighted by the threatened innocence of the child in such a scene, is undercut by the force of her realist representation which so powerfully naturalises the situation that there seems no opportunity for the reader to question the way things are. The empirical verisimilitude functions perhaps to imply that human weakness and vice have always injured the vulnerable and innocent and always will. Adorno's criticisms of realist writing are formidable and have remained influential within subsequent critical perspectives. Nevertheless, as with his attack on Enlightenment modes of thought more generally, there remains some ambiguity in his arguments against realism and in favour of modernism in that he aligns the fiction of Honoré de Balzac (1799–1850) and Charles Dickens (1812–70) with that of modernism (Taylor 1980: 163).

This ambivalence towards the Enlightenment and the associated form of literary realism is even more marked in the writing of another associate of the Frankfurt School, Walter Benjamin (1892–1940). Benjamin's imaginative responsiveness to the stuff of modern life is remarkably similar to the gusto of realist writers like Dickens and Balzac both in their appetite for and hatred of the proliferating materialism of their age. Moreover, Benjamin, on the whole, avoids the binary polarisation that sets up a progressive modernism against a conservative realism. Benjamin is perceptive in recognising the more significant continuities between certain kinds of realism and modernism. The great hero of modernism for Benjamin is Charles Baudelaire (1821–67) whose lyric poetry gives dramatic voice to the shock and alienation that characterised the first impact of mass urban society around the middle of the nineteenth century. More accurately perhaps, Benjamin recognised in the personae of Baudelaire's poems, a new type of the modern hero and writer: a type fascinated yet repelled by the heterogeneity and spectacle of city streets, always aloof and isolated in the midst of the crowd. This modernist urban hero is part dandy, part *flâneur* or boulevard-saunterer, part detective, part criminal, Benjamin argues (Benjamin [1955–71] 1983: 40–1). He connects this kind of hero with the cunning watchfulness that the North American writer James Fenimore Cooper (1789–1851) had represented in his apache characters in his popular Mohican stories of the American wilderness. That relentless attention to the smallest detail as a source of knowledge is transferred to the city apache to whom the 'pedestrians, the shops, the hired coaches, or a man leaning against a window' have the same burning interest as 'an immobile canoe or a floating leaf' in one of Cooper's stories (Benjamin [1955–71] 1983: 42).

Like Adorno, Benjamin associates the force of modernist writing with its shock effect that defamiliarises a habitual, customary response to reality (Benjamin [1955–71] 1983: 117). However, Benjamin, in his study of Baudelaire, embeds the practice of writing much more profoundly and inseparably than Adorno in the economics and materiality of the life of its era: in the new glamour of consumerism, in the threatening electric energy sensed in the agitated, amorphous city crowds, in the squalor and precariousness of urban poverty. Benjamin pays tribute to Baudelaire's supreme poetic expression of this modernist response to mass society but he sees Baudelaire as working in the same tradition as writers like Balzac and Dickens who are usually regarded as nineteenth-century realists. Benjamin quotes Dickens's complaint that he cannot write without the imaginative resource of London streets: 'It seems as if they supplied something to my brain, which it cannot bear, when busy to lose. For a week or a fortnight I can write prodigiously in a retired place...and a day in London sets me up again and starts me. But the toil and labour of writing, day after day, without that magic lantern, is *immense*....My figures seem disposed to stagnate without crowds about them' (Benjamin [1955–71] 1983: 49). (The source of this quotation is Forster 1892: 317.)

Benjamin shares the critical perspective of the Frankfurt School towards the culture industry and the negative perception of society as increasingly dominated by mass production, consumerism and bureaucracy. He recognises in mass produced cheap literature and in the new popular cinema powerful forces for an induced moral and cultural conformity and for frivolous distraction from real social problems. Yet the language in which he speaks about modern urban life has little of Adorno's disdainful austerity. (Benjamin's essay 'The Work of Art in the Age of Mechanical Reproduction' provides one of the fullest expressions of his complex response to mass consumption and production. See Benjamin [1955] 1999: 211–44.) In *Charles Baudelaire* Benjamin writes of mass production, 'The more industry progresses, the more perfect are the imitations which it throws on the market. The commodity is bathed in a profane glow' (Benjamin [1955–71] 1983: 105). Benjamin writes so perceptively about commodity culture because he is susceptible to its specious, profane glamour. This mixture of horror and attraction for the materiality of the modern world is an ambivalence he shares not only with Baudelaire but also with the great realist writers. His typically detailed observation of the preference of the bourgeoisie for things made of plush and velvet fabrics which preserve the impression of every touch, would have delighted Dickens (Benjamin [1955–71] 1983: 46). Moreover, Benjamin regards popular forms of writing like Fenimore Cooper's adventure stories and Edgar Allan Poe's (1809–49) detective fiction, both forms that became the staple of a mass-produced realist mode of literature, with real appreciation, recognising the relevance of their formal and thematic qualities to modern existence. In this openness to the progressive potential of different generic forms of creative realist expression and in his responsiveness to the sensual material substance of reality, Benjamin is not unlike the persona of the writer he recognises in Baudelaire's image of the rag-picker who sifts the daily city waste for his livelihood. Such an attitude, constituting an absorbed, unfastidious connoisseurship towards the materiality of existence offers a useful way of understanding part of the artistic impulse behind realism: a complex, ambivalent responsiveness towards, rather than repulsion from, the tangible stuff of reality. Realism is committed to the material actuality we share as embodied creatures.

2

REALISM, ANTI-REALISM AND POSTMODERNISM

What modernist writers largely rebelled against in the texts of their nineteenth-century predecessors was what they saw as the complacent moral certainty and over-rational coherence that seemed to underpin plot structure, narrative perspective and characterisation in realist novels. They did not, by and large, reject the very possibility that literary art could produce some form of knowledge of reality, however elusive and uncircumscribed the real had come to seem. During the second half of the twentieth century, however, a new theoretical understanding of what constitutes reality developed, undermining far more radically the rational grounds of Enlightenment values and the expressive form of realism. This new perspective was both anti-realism and **anti-humanism**. The new paradigm wholly rejects the human capacity for knowledge creation, recognising instead the constituting force of an impersonal system of language to construct the only sense of reality we can ever achieve. Our intuitive, commonsensical view of language is that words refer to a pre-existing reality beyond linguistics; words are the means by which we transmit or reproduce experience and knowledge of the physical and social worlds. Clearly this is the view of language informing the narrative voice of *Daniel Deronda* with its confidently detailed account of a specific social world. In this sense, language tends to be thought of as somehow transparent; we look through the words, as it were, to the actuality they point to.

FROM STRUCTURALISM TO POSTSTRUCTURALISM AND POSTMODERNISM

This unquestioning acceptance of what we can call the referential capacity of language to offer us access to the extra-linguistic world was undermined by the structural linguistics developed by Swiss semiologist, Ferdinand de Saussure (1857–1913), in the early years of the twentieth century (Saussure [1916] 1983). At the centre of Saussurian linguistics is the counter-intuitive claim that words are meaningful, not because they refer to things in the world, but because of their relationship with other words. The most easily grasped example of this structuralist thinking is the case of binary oppositions. No understanding of the concept 'short' is possible in the absence of the concept 'long'. The meaning of both words is produced by their structural relationship of difference. The same interdependent structure produces the meaning of those binary concepts that form the major framework of categories by which we think: good and evil, beautiful and ugly, above and below, light and dark, nature and culture, enlightenment and ignorance, right and wrong, and so on. The relationship of all words to the actual world, Saussure argues, is arbitrary and accidental. If there were some inherent, necessary connection between the written form or the sound of 'good' and its meaning, then the word (or **sign** as Saussure calls it) would have to be identical everywhere, in all languages, which is clearly not the case. Language is a closed system that produces meaning from its own internal relationships. This is so for even the most basic unit of sound: human beings can only acquire speech because they have the ability to recognise difference, to distinguish 't' from 'd' from 'b'. Language is constituted as a system of differences at the micro and macro levels.

Where does this radical view of language leave realist fiction with its implicit claim to use words to produce an accurate imitation of the real world? What we might notice, looking again at the opening of *Daniel Deronda* from a structuralist perspective, is Eliot's reliance on binary oppositions to produce her meaning. The questions of the first paragraph are structured overtly upon conceptual oppositions, but in the second paragraph, also, gambling 'in the open air under a southern sky' produces most of the negative force accruing to the contrary image of the condensation of human breath in the enclosed luxury of fashionable resorts. The reader's responsiveness to this passage is achieved by this internal relationship within the paragraph itself rather than by checking personal knowledge of nineteenth-century gambling resorts and con- firming the empirical correspondence of the words to external reality. The image of the child in the third paragraph summons up the binary moral categories of innocence and experience upon which the meaning of the chapter as a whole depends, hence its title 'The Spoiled Child'. In this way, Eliot's novel can be thought of as a closed linguistic struc- ture that produces its own meaning system independent of any accu- rate, referential correspondence to external reality. From approximately the 1960s into the 1980s this kind of formal structuralist approach to narratives of all kinds provided a dominant critical method and I shall return to this in more detail in Part III.

The radical import of structural linguistics consisted of its logical severing of words from the world, but, in other ways, structuralism can be understood as part of the Enlightenment project of producing sys- tematic knowledge. The ideal driving structuralism was the success of natural sciences like physics and chemistry which had reduced the immense multitudinous physical properties of *things* to the simplicity of a few basic chemical elements whose structural relationships could account for the diversity of forms the material world assumed. By anal- ogy, structural linguists hoped to arrive at a basic elemental grammar or system of rules that would be able to show how the infinite number of verbal variations apparent in the social world were produced. The scien- tific search for this basic grammar (termed *langue*) underlying all verbal forms (termed *parole*) has proved elusive. It was the radical aspect of structuralism, as it turned out, that had an ambitious and exciting future. The various strands of this development of structuralist logic are brought together under the umbrella term 'poststructuralism'. What these various forms of poststructuralism share is a concern to think through the implications of the structuralist account of language in the broader terms of culture and history. The advent of structuralism is sometimes referred to as the 'linguistic turn' and poststructuralism as the 'cultural turn'. Since the 1980s the 'cultural turn' has produced some of the most challenging and rigorous accounts of social structures, ideological processes and cultural productions. In what follows I shall deal largely with those aspects of poststructuralism that are most directly related to an understanding of realism.

The optimistic humanist ideals of Enlightenment are based on the belief; that intellectual and empirical observation of subjective and material realities produces an objective knowledge of the world which, together with rational morality, propels human progress. This optimism cannot logically survive an acceptance of the constructive function of language. Language does not serve as a neutral or translucent means of communication. All human beings are born into an already existing system of meaning and they can only ever 'know' reality by means of the conceptual categories their language system allows them. As an illustrative example, think of the ways in which we order our understanding of and response to the furry, four-footed creatures with which we share geography: pets, wild life, game, vermin, pests, meat. Yet these categorising words are cultural meanings and values by which we classify the creatures, not intrinsic qualities that they bear with them straight from the hand of god or nature. The conceptual and classifying structure of language is the bearer of values as well as meanings and we cannot operate the meaning system without at the same time activating the values. The **grand narratives** of Enlightenment thought, with their ideals of human progress and a just community dependent upon the sovereign power of rational knowledge and moral judgement, can themselves be seen as a fiction or illusion produced by language; they are a cultural and linguistic construct. The term 'enlightenment' derives value and meaning from its structural relationship to the concept of 'ignorance' but these classifying values are attributed to what is actually a continuum of human skills and cultural activities as arbitrarily as the terms 'pets' and 'pests' are used to classify the animal kingdom. Similarly the terms 'rational' and 'irrational', 'moral' and 'immoral' are cultural categories that we impose on the continuum of human behaviour and thought; they are not inherent meanings by which we know the world objectively. Even the subjective self, the sovereign location of rationality and moral discrimination, can only know its 'self' by means of the language system into which it is born. Without the pronoun 'I' as a binary opposition to 'you', how could a sense of unique self identity be achieved? Yet everyone refers to themself as 'I'.

It is easy to see the extent to which realist fiction both depends upon and supports the illusion of the underlying Enlightenment narrative.

Novelistic language purports to correspond faithfully to the social and physical worlds, the realist plot is typically structured upon the epistemological progress of readers and principal characters from ignorance to knowledge, and characterisation normally focuses upon the highly individualised inner subjective self-development of rational understanding and moral discrimination. This movement of the novel towards the resolution of mysteries and difficulties produces a reassuring sense of closure, an affirmation that life, understood in its totality, forms a meaningful pattern. Let us compare this traditional form of novel with the opening of a novel that expresses a postmodern perception and is informed by an understanding of poststructural thinking. Here are the first paragraphs of Angela Carter's (1940–1992) *Nights at the Circus* (1984), which, like *Daniel Deronda*, begins with a young man attempting to gain knowledge of the central female protagonist. But what kind of epistemology underwrites the aesthetics of this passage?

> 'Lor' love you, sir!' Fevvers sang out in a voice that clanged like dustbin lids. 'As to my place of birth, why, I fancy I first saw light of day right here in smoky old London, didn't I! Not billed the 'Cockney Venus', for nothing, sir, though they could just as well 'ave called me 'Helen of the Hire Wire', due to the unusual circumstances in which I come ashore – for I never docked via what you might call *normal channels*, sir, oh, dear me, no; but, just like Helen of Troy, was *hatched*.'
>
> 'Hatched out of a bloody great egg while Bow Bells rang, as ever is!' The blonde guffawed uproariously, slapped the marbly thigh on which her wrap fell open and flashed a pair of vast, blue, indecorous eyes at the young reporter with his open notebook and his poised pencil, as if to dare him: 'Believe it or not!' Then she spun round on her swivelling dressing-stool – it was a plush-topped, backless piano stool, lifted from the rehearsal room – and confronted herself with a grin in the mirror as she ripped six inches of false lash from her left eyelid with an incisive gesture and a small, explosive, rasping sound.
>
> Fevvers, the most famous *aerialiste* of her day; her slogan, 'Is she fact or is she fiction?' And she didn't let you forget it for a minute; this query, in the French language, in foot-high letters, blazed forth from a wall-sized poster, souvenir of her Parisian triumphs, dominating her

London dressing-room. Something hectic, something fittingly impetuous and dashing about that poster, the preposterous depiction of a young woman shooting up like a rocket, whee! In a burst of agitated sawdust towards an unseen trapeze somewhere above in the wooden heavens of the Cirque d'Hiver. The artist had chosen to depict her ascent from behind – bums aloft, you might say; up she goes, in a steatopygous perspective, shaking out about her those tremendous red and purple pinions, pinions large enough, powerful enough to bear up such a big girl as she. And she was a *big* girl.

(Carter 1984: 7)

This writing constitutes a radical challenge to any notion of verifiable truth as an evaluative criterion of good fiction. The question of moral categorisation that opens *Daniel Deronda* ('was the good or evil dominant') is replaced by the query, 'Is she fact or is she fiction?' It is immediately obvious that the whole point of the passage is to keep this uncertainty in oscillation. Not only does Fevvers reject the normal empirical origin in a biological family history, she is quite openly telling stories about herself: 'I fancy I first saw the light of day'. She constructs self identity as a performance that is as extravagantly artificial as the six inches of false eye-lash that she rips off so theatrically. Her being defies epistemological definition: she operates across the boundaries of fact and fiction, myth and reality, human and supernatural. The binary either/or alternatives that open *Daniel Deronda* have no purchase in this scheme of things. The references to Helen of Troy, Venus and the wall-size poster of Fevvers in upward flight upon huge red and purple wings suggest the way notions of identity are ultimately dependent upon cultural narratives and images. Birth is not the unique originating point of who we are; rather a self is produced by the stories of self through which we interpret our lives. This **textuality** of identity, the constructive power of cultural texts and fictions to produce the notion of self, operates most obviously at the level of stereotypes like the dumb blonde, the warm-hearted cockney whore, woman as chaste angel or divinity; all of these fictions are jokingly evoked in the introductory representation of the novel's heroine, Fevvers.

THE POSTSTRUCTURAL CRITIQUE OF REALISM

This open acknowledgement of the fictionality of all 'knowledge', the insistence that reality amounts to cultural stories and interpretations that we impose upon existence to create meaning for ourselves and of ourselves is the most typical characteristic of postmodern writing. It is, needless to say, directly contrary to the implicit epistemological claims of realist writing to convey knowledge about the extra-linguistic world. *Nights at the Circus* is also postmodern in its pervasive use of parody and burlesque to mock the conventional cultural order that attempts to hold in place stereotypical moral and social binary oppositions and the ideological values they perpetuate. Equally postmodern is the concern with commodification and repeatability: Fevvers presents herself as a product for public consumption while the notion of being hatched from an egg suggests simultaneously a non-human uniqueness and an infinite reproduction of sameness. We should finally note the playfulness of the language: the double entendres like 'normal channels', the dip and swoop of lexicon from 'bums aloft' to 'steatopygous perspective', the energised vitality of the syntax. Carter is not using words as self-effacing transmitters of knowledge; all of the qualities of her prose combine to foreground the textuality of the text, the delightful sensual materiality of the words themselves.

The poststructuralist French philosopher Jean-François Lyotard (1924–1998) has been an influential critic of what he calls the grand narrative of Enlightenment with its legitimisation of systematic, totalising forms of knowledge and its ideology of rational progress. In articulating this critique, Lyotard positions himself within the tradition of the Frankfurt School and its negative analysis of the Enlightenment for pursuing an instrumental form of knowledge as mastery of things and people. Lyotard ignores the ambivalence of writers like Adorno towards the Enlightenment and is actively hostile to Jürgen Habermas who went on to develop a more positive account.

Following Adorno, Lyotard criticises realism for its ideological and aesthetic conservatism. Realist art in the era of late capitalism, can no longer evoke reality, he claims, but it feeds the nostalgic desire for a world of moral certainties and experiential coherence, a world that can be grasped and known as a totality. The task assigned to realism, he says, is 'to preserve certain consciousnesses from doubt' (Lyotard [1979] 1984: 74). It fulfils this task, he argues, by drawing upon language, syntax, images and narrative sequences that the reader is familiar with and can easily decode to produce a reassuring interpretation of reality in terms of predictability, unity, simplicity and communicability. What this kind of realist representation veils is the anarchic postmodern condition of the late capitalist world. This constitutes a social universe ruled by global markets and a communication explosion based on computer technology, situated in a physical world of relativity, chaos theory and particle physics rather than the old predictable Newtonian narrative of cause and effect. These forces produce a postmodern culture of anti-realism dominated by visual surface, simulation, fictionality, repetition, and the instantaneous. Images of war and disaster flash around the world in seconds but there is no way of separating their quality as ideological presentation from their correspondence to any actuality. Conflicts are fought out in high-tech media images as well as high-tech weaponry. A financial rumour circulating in Chicago can close down factories in Taiwan. The lives of media stars, performed in the glare of global publicity, blur inseparably into the fictional world of soaps. The Enlightenment narrative of knowledge as progressive understanding is redundant in an anti-realist culture of simulation and transitory identities. Yet Lyotard suggests that there is a positive potential here in the destruction of the basis of traditional forms of authority and power. The dominating Enlightenment grand narrative of rational progress and mastery, and associated realist expression, can he argues, be replaced by little narratives, local truths, unfinished meanings. Like Fevvers, we can refuse the conventional **humanism** type of life narrative of rational and moral development and instead create and perform our own instantaneous little histories making a playful burlesque out of all the cultural fictions available to us. For Lyotard the aesthetic form and underlying cognitive beliefs of realism are utterly incapable of representing the antirealism and antihumanism of the postmodern condition. Only avant-garde writing like Carter's can provide 'knowledge' of the random, multiplying, synthetic hyper-reality that is late capitalism. Yet, if this is the case, it could be argued against Lyotard that Carter is a modern realist still writing within the paradigm that knowledge of the extra-textual world can be produced and communicated. Literary genres do not stand still; to remain vibrant they adapt to the changing social realities within which they are produced. We might also just note in passing that George Eliot's similation of consumer-driven speculative capitalism to a gambling casino would seem also to foreground unpredictability as a structural force of the modern condition. David Harvey, a leading theorist of postmodern culture, has termed the speculative finance of late capitalism, the 'casino economy' (Harvey 1990: 332).

The French literary critic, Roland Barthes (1915–80), also castigates realist novelists for representing a world 'purged of the uncertainty of existence' (Barthes [1953] 1967: 27). 'For all the great storytellers of the nineteenth century, the world may be full of pathos but it is not derelict,' he writes (Barthes [1953] 1967: 28). By this, Barthes means that human life and characters, as represented in realist fiction, may be given the sombre colour of intense suffering and catastrophe but, within such fiction, life and human identity are never denied all meaning and purpose. A consoling sense of pattern or closure is never finally refused. Barthes labels those kinds of novels that provide such reassurance, *readerly* (Barthes [1973] 1990: 4). He associates this kind of writing with mass commodity culture. The **readerly** work offers itself to the reader to be passively consumed, he says. It demands only an acquiescent acceptance of its predictable, familiar representation of character and plot. Such products, Barthes claims, 'make up the enormous mass of our literature' (Barthes [1973] 1990: 5). Complicity with consumerism is not the only role of such reassuring realism; Barthes argues that it has a yet more insidious ideological effect. Despite the great variety of characters and the many different plots that novels offer their readers, a basic framework of conceptual beliefs about human life is continually reasserted. For example, the binary oppositions that insist that male is only and always different from female, black from white, rich from poor, west from east, are continually reiterated, as is the hierarchical predominance of the first term over the second in each of these pairs. Realist novels present these value as if they were universal attributes of an unchanging human nature. Barthes claims that this kind of writing allowed the 'triumphant bourgeoisie of the last century...to look upon its values as universal and to carry over to sections of society which were absolutely heterogeneous to it all the Names which were part of its ethos' (Barthes [1953] 1967: 29). What Barthes is suggesting here is that realist novels were complicit in fostering the confidence with which European nations imposed their understanding of moral identity and values upon colonised peoples, claiming, and often believing, they were upholding abiding human laws and promoting enlightenment and progress. This perception of the eurocentric values of realist writing has been radically developed by critics like Edward Said (1935–), Gayatri Spivak (1924–) and Bill Ashcroft, who writing from the perspective of postcolonial countries point out, among other things, the way a colonial education system offered native peoples 'great literature', as part of its civilising mission; a literature which included adventure stories of noble British heroes fighting for the honour of their country and the purity of their women against perfidious, superstitious and bestial 'natives' (See, for example, Bill Ashcroft *et al.* 1989; Said 1984 and 1994; Spivak 1988; Azim 1993.)

Barthes contrasts what he terms *writerly* texts to the complacent gender and racial ideologies of the **classic realist** story. *Writerly* texts have to be actively produced by the reader rather than consumed, so that the reader in this sense 'writes' the text in the act of reading. Barthes' thinking is drawing upon the structuralist insight that language is a system of differences, that signs (words) acquire meaning only by means of their relationship to other signs (words). Saussure had shown how signs are composed of two elements: a signifier comprising a sound or visual mark and a signified, comprising the concept culturally associated with the signifier. Yet there is no necessary and fixed relationship between signifier and signified, and a single signifier can slide across a wide chain of meaning. In *Nights at the Circus*, Fevvers declares 'I never docked via what you might call *normal channels*'. The phrase 'normal channels' usually signifies a proper or official way of doings things in a bureaucratic context. Fevvers is sliding the meaning humorously across to accommodate the concept of normal birth via an anatomical canal. But canals and channels also suggest water, hence the idea of docking, and this in turn plays upon the nineteenth-century euphemism for birth as a little boat bearing a baby over the ocean. This propels a further spillage of meaning into the myth of Venus arising from the water. All of these connotations are brought into play by Carter as part of the unorthodox plurality that is her heroine. Barthes uses the terms 'text' and 'textuality' to suggest the interwoven, many layered quality of this kind of writing. For Barthes, writerly texts are those that exploit the proliferation of the signifying chain, thereby shaking the assumed stability of conceptual meaning. Such writing, he claims, is potentially revolutionary, subverting social orthodoxies and breaching cultural taboos. The ideal text he says is 'a galaxy of signifiers, not a structure of signifieds' (Barthes [1973] 1990: 5) and the ideal reading aims to recognise that 'everything signifies ceaselessly and several times' (Barthes [1973] 1990: 12).

However, despite this insistence upon distinguishing readerly realist works from writerly experimental texts, Barthes' own brilliant writerly reading of Balzac's story, *Sarrasine* (1830), suggests that it may not be realist narratives *per se* that can be categorised as imposing closed unitary meaning. What may be at stake is the way in which we chose to read any piece of writing. You may have noticed already how conveniently I have been able to turn to the passage from *Daniel Deronda* to illustrate most of the points I have been making. This is not just a case of having carefully chosen a novel that would let me have my cake and eat it. Texts of all kinds prove very hospitable to the meanings readers seek to find in them.

DECONSTRUCTING REALISM

Barthes' emphasis upon play and textuality draws upon the work of French philosopher, Jacques Derrida (1930–). Derrida's deconstructive method has exerted a very powerful influence upon current literary criticism, especially as practised in America. His project has been no less than the deconstruction of the whole tradition of Western thought and what he calls its metaphysics of presence. In this sense at least, Derrida can be seen as operating within the Enlightenment tradition which seeks to free human intellect by demystifying superstitious beliefs and secularising the sacred. He shows, by means of meticulously detailed readings of philosophical texts from Plato to Nietzsche, Heidegger and Husserl, how speech has been consistently valued as more authentic than writing. This is because the meaning and truth of speech is held to be more immediately in touch with an originating thought or intention than writing is. Truth, in Western philosophy, has always been understood to be guaranteed by presence: of an author, or a mind, or God.

Writing is seen as secondary or supplementary to speech in that it is at least two removes from an originating and authenticating presence. This 'metaphysics of presence' underpins an ideal of Truth as whole and unitary, and of meaning as fixed, stable and definitive. It also provides the basis of a conceptual hierarchy which values speech over writing, presence over absence, the spiritual over the material, the original over the copy, the same over difference. Derrida calls this Western structure of thought, logocentrism. Derrida's deconstruction of these hierarchies begins from the Saussurian sense of language as an impersonal system of differences. Yet Derrida takes the logic of this insight much further than Saussure ever envisaged. Saussure theorised signs as composed of a signifier and a signified, that is a mental concept, but Derrida claims that a signifier cannot be arrested in a single meaning that is present in the mind. Signifiers refer only to other signifiers in an unstoppable motion. Thus language must be understood as a signifying practice in which meaning is constantly deferred.

Let us take a rather simple way of demonstrating this complex idea. The signifier 'evil' depends upon the binary relationship with the signifier 'good' for its signified meaning and vice versa. Yet logically this entails that neither meaning exists positively in its own right. Each signifier must point perpetually to its opposite in an unstable oscillation that can never cease. The same structural interdependence ensures that any definitive meaning of the word 'fact' is continually deferred by its necessary relationship of difference to 'fiction'. But these are only micro examples of the general condition of being of language: the very possibility of language is founded upon difference. Derrida describes language as a field of infinite substitutions (Derrida [1967] 1978: 289). He says, 'the meaning of meaning (in the general sense of meaning...) is infinite implication, the indefinite referral of signifier to signifier' (Derrida [1967] 1978: 25). Derrida uses the word 'dissemination' to evoke this notion of language as spillage and spread of meaning without closure or end and he coins the term *différance* from the French verb '*différer*', meaning both to differ and to defer, to bring together the ideas that language is a system of difference in which meaning is always deferred.

By affirming language as *différance*, Derrida totally rejects the ideal of Truth enshrined in all forms of logocentrism. Traditional critical studies of realist novels have been based upon implicit logocentric beliefs: critics assume that the writing expresses the author's intention which constitutes the 'real truth' or 'essential meaning' of the story, or the 'truth' of the fiction is understood as guaranteed by the accurate correspondence of the words to an authentic objective reality beyond the text. One of Derrida's most quoted remarks is *'Il n'y a pas de hors texte'* (Derrida [1967] 1976: 163). This is sometimes taken as a denial that there is any reality at all beyond texts and textuality, beyond those interpretations or fictions imposed on us by our language system. However, rather than asserting that there is no reality apart from texts, Derrida might more reasonably be taken to claim that there is no out-side-text. In other words, there is no authority beyond the writing itself, whether that authority be thought of as the author, God, science, objectivity, that can guarantee its 'truth'. Derrida perceives language as an impersonal creative energy that exists quite independently of any intention of an author or speaker.

Derrida calls this energy that constitutes writing 'force' or 'play'. He writes, 'There is not a single signified that escapes, even if recaptured, the play of signifying references that constitute language. The advent of writing is the advent of this play' (Derrida [1967] 1976: 7). Derrida also suggests that forms of avant-garde writing consciously elaborate a practice of writing as infinite play of meaning rather than deploying language as a medium for conveying an authorial truth or attempting an accurate imitation of a pre-existing, non-linguistic objective reality. This notion of the playful deferral of meaning has been immensely influential on critical practice and on literary postmodern writing, especially in North America.

However, despite his affirmation of language as limitless play, Derrida, himself, continues to insist upon the necessity for rational discourse, especially on the part of the critic. He argues that it is through 'a careful and thorough discourse', brought to bear upon any particular text, that a critic comes to discover 'the crevice through which the yet unnameable glitter beyond the closure can be glimpsed' (Derrida [1967] 1976: 14). His deconstructive method consists of a 'certain way of reading' (Derrida [1967] 1978: 288), which brings to light those points in the text where the language seems to escape its own closure, where images, metaphors and phrases function to put into doubt the meaning that the writing seems elsewhere to assert. Derrida is mainly referring to the kind of critical reading that should be brought to the study of philosophical texts but there is no reason why the same approach should not be brought to literary texts in general and to realist texts in particular. By means of 'a certain kind of reading', perhaps realist writing too can be shown to contain crevices glittering with a play of meaning that explodes their apparent closure.

Before moving on to an example of a deconstructive reading of realist writing that aims to do just this, it may be helpful to summarise the critique of realism produced by those three 'isms' of modernism, postmodernism and poststructuralism. At the heart of this critique is a rejection of the Enlightenment view of rational knowledge and human progress. Far from producing new understanding of the world, realist novels are accused of colluding with functional reason to produce philistine readerly narratives. These give comfort to the reader's moral and cultural expectations of what life should be like rather than challenging the existing conceptual and socio-political status quo. Even when graphic accounts of suffering and injustice are represented, the effect of the surface verisimilitude of realist form is to naturalise such happenings as part of the inevitable condition of human existence. This universalising tendency has also functioned to underpin European bourgeois morality and individualism as timeless values to be imposed upon the rest of the world. With the full development of the postmodern condition, the aesthetic and cognitive bankruptcy of realism is confirmed; even popular culture is currently abandoning realism as a mode of expression. This is a formidable charge sheet against realism, but, as we have seen, co-existing with this critique there have been elements of unease at thus dismissing the near century of literary achievement constituted in the novels of writers like Dickens, Eliot, Balzac, and Tolstoy. A way of circumventing this embarrassment is that suggested by Barthes' reading of Balzac's novella, *Sarrasine*, and Derrida's deconstructive method. 'A certain kind of reading' can be used to liberate so-called realist writers from accusations of linguistic and cognitive complacency by demonstrating that their writing is covertly proto-poststructuralist, experimental, sceptical, and self-reflexive. The limitation of this liberation approach, which aims to free realism from its own entrapment, is that it perpetuates the rather unhelpful dominant critical binarism that constitutes the experimental as progressive, open and good and realism as conservative, restrictive and bad art. It thus functions to inhibit genuinely new thinking about realism that might move understanding on beyond the current assumptions.

Let us now look at a typical deconstructive reading of a realist text by J. Hillis Miller (1928–), one of a group of American literary critics, including Paul de Man (1919–1983) at Yale University, who have been strongly influenced by Jacques Derrida. Paul de Man's most influential text is *Blindness and Insight* (1983), and central to the Yale deconstructionist approach is the notion that frequently a text's blindness to logical inconsistencies within its discourse is, in fact, the site of its most profound insights. These points of illuminating blindness are very often revealed by means of a close critical reading of the writer's use of rhetorical tropes and figurative language. From this perspective it is significant to my argument that throughout his essay on 'The Fiction of Realism: *Sketches by Boz, Oliver Twist,* and Cruikshank's Illustrations', Miller returns continually to the binary trope of liberation versus entrapment (Miller 1971: 85–153). He opens his discussion by pointing out that structural linguistics has brought about the 'disintegration' of the realist paradigm which holds that a literary text is 'validated by its one-to-one correspondence to some social, historical, or psychological reality' (Miller 1971: 85). He goes on to argue, however, that while realist texts may invite readers to interpret stories according to this paradigm, they also provide openings for another kind of reading. *Sketches by Boz* (1836–7), Miller suggests, is a particularly challenging text on which to test this claim, that realist texts offer deconstructive insights into their own realist blindness, since the writing seems very firmly rooted in Dickens's journalistic mode. Comprised of highly detailed sketches of London streets, people and ways of living, 'here, even if nowhere else, Dickens seems to have been practising a straightforward mimetic realism' (Miller 1971: 86–7). The fallacy that realism offers an accurate correspondence to external reality 'here…affirms itself in the sunlight with a clear conscience' (Miller 1971: 89). And he points out that the whole tradition of critical response to *Sketches by Boz* has similarly affirmed this fallacy in praising the *Sketches* for their fidelity to the real.

The main strategy by which Dickens's writing in *Sketches by Boz* inveigles the unwary reader into a realist interpretation is the recurrent use of metonymic contiguity. Metonymy is a figure of speech in which the part stands in for the whole to which it belongs, as in the phrase 'all hands on deck'. 'Hands' in this expression refers to the whole body and person to which the hands are joined or contiguous. Our normal experience of reality accords to metonymic contiguity. In focusing upon Dickens's use of metonymy, Miller is drawing upon the work of linguist Roman Jakobson (1896–1982) whose theories will be discussed in more detail in Chapter 3. As I walk across a room or down a street, for example, I experience space and time in terms of adjacency and continuity: one shop moves me on to the adjacent one and one moment of window gazing flows into the next. I take this small part of my experience of the world as standing in metonymically for the whole which extends contiguously from it in like manner. In *Sketches by Boz*, the narrator typically describes his progress down a street, moving contiguously from one spectacle to the next. In addition, Boz frequently pursues an imaginary contiguous progression in which he moves from some perceived detail of a character's clothes or behaviour to speculation about the whole personality and thence to the even larger whole of the person's life. This narrative pattern of metonymic progression, Miller argues, mimics one of the underlying assumptions of realism that there is 'a necessary similarity between a man, his environment, and the life he is forced to lead within that environment' (Miller 1971: 98). It is by means of these rhetorical strategies, Miller says, that Dickens's writing entraps the naive reader into a readerly consumption of the text as mimetically 'true to life'.

However, for a discriminating reader, able to espouse the kind of detached distance that Miller attributes to Boz, the text contains sufficient clues for a more insightful reading, one that performs an act of liberation from the illusion of realism. Miller claims, 'In several places Boz gives the reader the information he needs to free himself from a realistic interpretation' (Miller 1971: 119). This kind of discriminating reader is in sharp contrast both to the naive realist reader and the characters of the stories, most of whom, Miller claims, 'remain trapped in their illusions' (Miller 1971: 104). What the narrator indicates is that all the characters live their lives as some form of imitation; their behaviour, gestures and mannerisms are constantly likened in the text to those of theatre, pantomime and farce. 'Character after character in the *Sketches* is shown to be pretending to be what he is not', Miller claims, but they remain blindly unaware of this hollowness behind the surface display that is their entire existence (Miller 1971: 109). Only Boz and the perceptive reader recognise the fraudulence of social reality, the fictive nature of all social identities. For the mass of the urban inhabitants of London, as represented in *Sketches by Boz*, life is a sordid sham:

> People in the *Sketches* are trapped not by social forces but by human fabrications already there within which they must live their lives. They live not in free creativity but as stale repetitions of what has gone before. The world of the *Sketches* is caught in the copying of what preceded it. Each new form is a paler imitation of the past. Each person is confined in the tawdry imitation of stale gestures....They are pathetically without awareness that their cheapness is pathetic, hopelessly imprisoned within the cells of a fraudulent culture.
>
> (Miller 1971: 111)

Although Miller is ostensibly describing the fictionality of all human identities as represented in a fictional text, here, his language strikingly evokes the non-linguistic materiality of mass commodity production. Miller's own rhetoric transforms the urban poor, who crowd the pages of *Sketches*, into a mass-produced, unenlightened, cheap uniformity.

The critical act of revealing the fictitiousness of realist claims to correspond to a non-linguistic, extra-textual reality is not performed, Miller says, in pursuit of some truth beyond or behind the fictions that constitute society. 'Behind each fiction there is another fiction....No one can escape' (Miller 1971: 121). The only liberation possible from imprisonment in a fraudulent culture of repeated imitations of imitations is by means of the detached, aware playfulness cultivated by the artist and the intelligent critical reader. There is a striking similarity between the opposition Miller sets up between 'free creativity' on the one hand and, on the other, the 'tawdry imitation' of mere surface to which the mass of people are condemned and that antithesis found in Woolf's essays on realism in which she contrasts an 'uncircumscribed spirit' to realism's philistine materialism. Miller chooses *Sketches by Boz* as an uncompromisingly realist text for deconstruction. I have chosen to discuss Miller's essay for somewhat opposite reasons: it seems to me to offer a particularly clear insight into the blindness of much poststructuralist critical theory. As we have seen, one recurrent theme in the developing critique of realism, from modernism to a postmodern present, has been the accusation that realist writing supports a comforting conservatism: its form and content matches the naive reader's conventional expectations about the way things are. Yet does not the practice of deconstructive criticism offer its own form of seductive and flattering comfort? The reassurance of feeling above the crowd, more individual than the mass? Who would not want to recognise their self as that certain kind of discriminating reader, operating at a detached distance from those naive entrapped consumers of popular culture? A reader, moreover, who shares the liberating insight and playfulness of the artist? The tropes of freedom and enclosure that structure Miller's essay point to an underlying anxiety within the critical tradition I have traced in Part I: an almost visceral dread of the proliferating amorphousness of a mass culture. To escape immersion in this materiality, artists and intellectuals seek the spaciousness of an uncircumscribed playfulness. This is the ideology inscribed in the long critique of realism. To recognise this, however, is not to reject the radical insights of poststructuralism or to deny the forms of knowledge offered by experimental art. A proper understanding of realism, however, requires us to disentangle the insights of the critique from its ideological blindness.

Miller does not refer in his essay to one of the most overt statements the narrator of *Sketches* makes as to the relation of the writing to external reality. In giving an account of Newgate Prison, Boz disclaims 'any presumptuous confidence in our own descriptive powers' (Dickens [1836–7] 1995: 235). Moreover, he promises not to fatigue the reader with the kinds of details offered in authoritative statistical and empirical reports: 'We took no notes, made no memoranda, measured none of the yards...are unable even to report of how many apartments the gaol is composed' (Dickens [1836–7] 1995: 235). Clearly this writing is not seeking to inveigle the naive reader into a sense that they are about to be offered a one-to-one correspondence with existing reality. What most contemporary readers would have recognised here is Boz's rejection of the kinds of truth and accuracy that formed the basis of scientific claims to knowledge as mastery of the objective world. When Boz comes to refer to the condemned cell at Newgate, he makes a direct appeal not to empirical fact but to the reader's imagination: 'Conceive the situation of a man, spending his last night on earth in this cell' (Dickens [1836–7] 1995: 243). This invitation to a shared understanding of what would be entailed in such a situation is followed by an intensely imaginative representation of the anguish, dreams, false hopes and terror of such a man. Surely, it is immensely condescending to assume that most of Boz's nineteenth-century readers would have naively confused his appeal to imaginative conjecture for an hour by hour factual account of some actual man's last night alive. Instead of subscribing to the currently dominant critical myth that realism naively claims to give its readers unmediated access to extra-linguistic reality, aiming at an impossible one-to-one fidelity between words and things, it will be more productive to think in terms of what I shall call referential generalisation. Boz's appeal to his readers to 'conceive the situation' can be understood as the founding invitation of realism and indeed of all communication. It is a gesture which openly admits to a specific referential absence, hence the need to conceive, to imagine, to represent. Yet the invitation is based upon an underlying grammar of consensual belief in the possibility of a shared communication about our experience and the world. This is the underlying grammar of community. As opposed to poststructuralism's grand liberation narrative into a discriminating realm of play, realism's contract with the reader is based upon the Enlightenment consensual belief in the possibility of a shared understanding. We might view both of these aspirations, Enlightenment's and poststructuralism's, as equally but oppositionally insightful and blind.

I conclude this chapter and Part I with a brief case study that sums up the shifting relationship of realism and experimentalism. It also helps us to see what is at stake in this long debate. Elaine Showalter's (1941–) publication of *A Literature of Their Own* (1978) could almost be said to have founded the whole enterprise of feminist criticism. In what was a ground-breaking study, Showalter brought to critical recognition the existence of a long tradition of women novelists who had been largely ignored in canonical perceptions of literary history. One of the achievements of this literature was its witness to women's struggle against patriarchal prejudice and injustice. In both their determination to write, despite hostile male commentary, and in the stories they told, women writers asserted the right for a literature and for lives of their own. Yet Showalter wrote rather unsympathetically of Virginia Woolf's significance within this tradition of women's writing (Showalter 1978: 263–97). Showalter claimed that Woolf's experimental style and subject matter precluded her from offering women readers positive realist representations of female identity that could serve as role models in the fight for greater social equality with men. Toril Moi's *Sexual Textual Politics* (1985) can be seen as another landmark text; this book was highly influential in introducing and fostering poststructural theory in Britain. In it, Toril Moi, a second generation feminist critic, took Showalter vigorously to task for her adherence to realism (Moi 1985: 1–8). Moi argued that experimental writers like Woolf challenged the conventional, common-sense binary division of gender inscribed in the language system. Her fiction, like that of other avant-garde writers, aimed to shatter the façade of empirical reality; thus it undermined the status quo of power structures far more radically than any amount of grimly detailed realist representations of women's suffering and exploitation. This kind of interpretive view has prevailed and the poststructuralist critical paradigm that Moi advocates has become the dominant evaluative orthodoxy: experimentalism is privileged over realism. The critical hierarchy is reversed but the binary structure remains in place. Whereas Showalter, working within realist values, had difficulty in adequately recognising Woolf's artistic achievement, current critical thinking has difficulty in fully accommodating and appreciating the writing of a novelist like Pat Barker (1943–) whose powerful novels, such as *Union Street* (1982) and *The Regeneration Trilogy* (1991–5), are written predominantly within a realist mode. Despite its radical themes and import, must we write off Barker's work as cognitively and aesthetically conservative and hence complicit with existing structures of authority and power? Or do we need to find some way of moving beyond the present limiting binarism that constitutes critical values?

For it is not only predominantly realist novels that cause critical embarrassment to the poststructural anti-realist paradigm. Arundhati Roy's (1961–) prize-winning novel, *The God of Small Things* (1999), with its deconstruction of binary identities and its self-consciously playful language, is clearly an experimental text. Yet in representing the brutal murder of an Untouchable in police custody, the writing emphasises the gruesome materiality of splintered bone, smashed teeth, broken flesh, choking blood by shifting into a realist mode. Is this to be read as a sudden conciliatory gesture to a naive desire for one-to-one correspondence between words and things so as to provide the illusion of a reassuringly familiar Eurocentric order of existence? This would obviously be an absurd interpretation. One solution to the problem might be to distinguish between the main European tradition of realist writing arising in the eighteenth and continuing throughout the nineteenth century on the one hand and, on the other, the less systematic adoption of a mode of realism by all kinds of writers at any historical period and in any culture. Yet this does not actually resolve the difficulty. The epistemology that underwrites all uses of realist representation is the same: the need to communicate information about the material, non-linguistic world. Thematically and formally, realism is defined by an imperative to bear witness to all the consequences, comic and tragic, of our necessarily embodied existence. Roy's description of police brutality is not primarily a fiction referring only to other fictions of atrocity. It invokes realism's humanist contract with the reader based upon the consensual belief that shared communication about material and subjective realities is possible. This, I have stressed, is also in large part the basis of community. We need an intelligent critical understanding of writing that aims to respond adequately to the materiality of existence in all its sensuous plushness and its bloodied flesh. It goes without saying that this understanding must also accommodate the recent insights of experimental writing and theory. Walter Benjamin's critical practice offers a model that is open and receptive to the whole range of cultural production and that recognises significant continuities between different genres and traditions rather than fixing them into binary opposition. With this in mind, I shall turn, in Part II, to the insights offered by the positive proponents of realism.

II

LITERARY REALISM
An Innovative Tradition

3

LITERARY REALISM IN NINETEENTH-CENTURY FRANCE

To move from the sustained critique of literary realism that I traced in Part I to the substantial body of positive writing on realism is to encounter a strikingly different view of the topic: there is not one unified form of realism but many. As with the term '**romanticism**', quite distinctive national histories and artistic conventions can easily be overlooked when realism is invoked in an over-simplified way. French, Russian, British, and American traditions of realism, to name but four, all developed somewhat differently under the impact of diverse national cultures and social forces. (Becker 1963: 3–38 surveys the different national developments of realism in his Introduction and provides documents on the subject from a wide range of countries.) The achievements of realist writing can only be fully understood within the specific context in which it was produced. Within the compass of Part II I have space only to look at the intertwined histories of French and British realist fiction during the nineteenth century. This is usually regarded as the great age of realism and France is also seen as the country in which the realist novel genre was most consciously pursued, debated, acclaimed and denounced throughout the century.

As this suggests, realist writing has not always been perceived as a conservative form, offering its readers a soothing view of reality that accords with moral, social and artistic conventions. On the contrary, as the Russian critic and philosopher of the novel, Mikhail Bakhtin

(1895–1975), has shown, the development of realism is propelled by radical experimentation with narrative technique. Bakhtin argues that the novel genre is essentially iconoclastic, subverting conventional literary forms and assimilating others: letters, diaries, journalism, fairy tale and **romance**. The history of literary realism is shaped by a protean restlessness and its dominant modes are those of comedy, irony and parody (Bakhtin 1981: 3–40). The Marxist critic of realism, György Lukács (1885–1971), also sees irony as inherent to realist form (Lukács [1914–15] 1978: 72–6). The novel genre undoubtedly gained popularity with a rapidly expanding bourgeois readership at a time when middle-class economic and political strengths were becoming dominant social forces, and by and large nineteenth-century novels tended to concern themselves with the values and life style of this class. However, the perspective offered in much nineteenth-century fiction was confrontational and critical rather than conciliatory. Bourgeois respectability, materialism and moral narrowness were the focus of ridicule more often than of praise. Moreover, as the century progressed, the novel continually widened the scope of its subject matter. As the critic Harry Levin says, 'The development of the novel runs parallel to the history of democracy, and results in a gradual extension of the literary franchise' (Levin 1963: 57). Erich Auerbach (1892–1957) in his classic study, *Mimesis: The Representation of Reality in Western Literature*, defines the central achievement of the development of realist writing from Homer to Virginia Woolf, as the 'serious treatment of everyday reality, [and] the rise of more extensive and socially inferior human groups to the position of subject matter' (Auerbach [1946] 1953: 491). Like most other major critics of realism, Auerbach sees the novel as the first literary form to develop a complex understanding of time as historical process and to find technical means within novelistic prose to represent this sense of temporality as it is experienced in individual lives.

Yet despite its innovatory energy, most historians of realism also stress its formal and thematic continuities with earlier and later literary forms. In *The Rise of the Novel*, Ian Watt, for example, situates the realist novel within an empirical philosophical tradition stretching from John Locke (1632–1704) to Bertrand Russell (1872–1970) and in a literary line from Cervantes (?1547–1616) to James Joyce (1882–1941) (Watt [1957] 1987: 21, 206, 292). Harry Levin sees the pictorial effect developed by

Émile Zola (1840–1902) as the forerunner of cinematic art and he also includes Marcel Proust (1871–1922), usually associated with early modernism, as the fifth realist writer within the main tradition of French realism (Levin 1963: 327). The influence of previous literary styles and conventions is part of the context in which we need to understand realism, but it is also important to locate literary history itself within the wider processes of economic, commercial, political, and cultural change. A helpful way of thinking about this is to understand the practice of writing as taking place within a **literary field**, that is, within a cultural space in which each writer must position him or herself in terms of choices of style, genre, readership, past traditions and future reputation. (Bourdieu 1996 provides a very full historicized account of the functioning of the literary field in nineteenth-century France.) Clearly this literary field is multiply interconnected with the much broader social field that is the location of economic, cultural and political power. For example, in France for much of the nineteenth century, poetry was regarded as the most prestigious literary form. The art of poetry was consecrated by long association with the sacred and spiritual. So the successful practice of poetry was rewarded with the highest amount of cultural capital or prestige. Yet the financial rewards of poetry were relatively low, so aspiring poets tended to come predominantly from a class wealthy enough to provide independent means of support. In contrast, the novel as a genre was held in low esteem in the early part of the century but financial rewards could be significant. Entry into the profession of novel writing was reasonably open to talent and did not require, as poetry did, a long formal education in literary tradition. As the century progressed, the expansion of cheap forms of mass publication and increases in literacy continually shifted the dynamics of the literary field and the choices of position it afforded would-be writers.

IDEALISM AND CLASSICAL THEORIES OF ART

Within the literary field in France, especially in the early decades of the nineteenth century, realist writers almost inevitably perceived themselves as taking an oppositional stance towards idealism. In brief, whereas realism derives from an acceptance that the objects of the world that we know by means of our sensory experience have an independent existence regardless of whether or not they are perceived or thought about, idealism gives primacy to the consciousness, or mind or spirit that apprehends. This privileging of the non-corporeal as the ultimate source of reality begins in the classical world with the teachings of Plato (428/427BC–348/347BC) and Aristotle (384–322BC) which together constitute a pervasive and powerful tradition within western notions of knowledge and aesthetics. (Williams 1965: 19–56 discusses the influence of classical views of the relationship of art and reality from the Renaissance into modern times.)

At the centre of Plato's philosophy is his concept of the Forms or Ideas. These he understands as eternal, transcendent realities that can only be directly comprehended by thought. Plato contrasts these Forms to the changeful, contingent world that constitutes our empirical existence. For example, we apprehend the notions of perfect justice and ideal beauty even though we never experience these phenomena in that perfection in our actual lives. Our knowledge of these ideals, therefore, Plato would argue, cannot derive from sensory information but rather comes from an intellectual intuition of the transcendent, universal Forms of Justice and Beauty. Platonist philosophy sees human beings as mediating between the two realms of the Ideal and the sensible. The human mind or soul can strive upwards and inwards towards an apprehension of the transcendent, incorporeal reality of the Forms, seeking union with an eternal Oneness that comprehends all Being. On the other hand, the physical instincts can obliterate these higher yearnings and human beings then live wholly within the limits of their biological nature or even degenerate into brutish creatures ruled by irrational passions and gross materialism. Plato entertained a poor opinion of artists as simply imitators of the sensible world which was itself only a poor imitation of the ideal Forms. Artistic representations for Plato were therefore at two removes from transcendent reality and in the *Republic* (360BC) he proposes that poets be excluded from the polis. Within the general currents of a Platonist tradition, however, as it became dispersed in western thought, the notion of spiritual apprehension of an ideal reality beyond the merely sensible world was very easily transmuted into a special claim for an artistic vision of perfection and timeless, universal truth.

Aristotelian thought rejects the mysticism of Platonic Forms. Aristotle was also more favourably inclined towards artistic representa-

tions, seeing imitation as central to the human capacity to learn. In the
Poetics (350BC) he notes:

> The general origin of poetry was due to two causes, each of them part
> of human nature. Imitation is natural to man from childhood, one of
> his advantages over the lower animals being this, that he is the most
> imitative creature in the world, and learns at first by imitation. And it
> is also natural for all to delight in works of imitation....The explana-
> tion is to be found in a further fact: to be learning something is the
> greatest of pleasures not only to the philosopher but also to the rest
> of mankind,...the reason of the delight in seeing the pictures is that it
> is at the same time learning – gathering the meaning of things.
>
> (Aristotle 1963: 8)

So for Aristotle, art, as imitation of the phenomenal world, is a form
of knowledge linked to pleasure; it is not, as it is for Plato, a dangerous distraction from a higher transcendent reality. But Aristotle does
somewhat complicate the way in which poets and artists fulfil their
function as knowledge producers. Although he understands the sensible world as the primary reality, he distinguishes between particular
phenomena and the universal categories to which we assign them as
part of the abstract ordering that structures our knowledge of the
world. So we recognise individuals as particular people but also know
them as sharing attributes that constitute the universal definition
'humanity'. Similarly with all else: we recognise particular things,
from a specific outburst of grief to an individual daisy, and simultaneously understand them in general terms as partaking of the universal
categories of 'grief' or 'emotion' and 'daisy' or 'flower'. Aristotle suggests that it is the poet's responsibility to represent the universal not
the particular. In this way the knowledge offered by art will have a
general, principled application not a contingent one that changes
from particular case to case:

> The poet's function is to describe, not the thing that has happened,
> but a kind of thing that might happen, i.e. what is possible as being
> probable or necessary....Hence poetry is something more philosophic

and of graver import than history, since its statements are of the nature of universals whereas those of history are singular.

(Aristotle 1963:17)

I shall suggest in Part III that the tension between particular historical reality and universal reality within literary realism is the means by which it conveys its own form of knowledge about the world.

The intermingling through time of Platonic and Aristotelian thought produced a classical view of art as nature perfected and as an intimation of timeless ideals. From this perspective, literary works were valued to the extent that they seemed to offer universal and enduring truths rather than local or particular perceptions of the world. In France, neo-classicism, a return to what was perceived as the aesthetic rules of antiquity, became, by the eighteenth century, an exacting standard against which all creative works were judged. Deviation from classical decorum put any rebellious writer or artist beyond the pale of public approval. The *Académie française*, a literary academy established in 1634 to regulate the standards of the French language, was at the centre of the institutionalisation and policing of an inflexible framework of literary conventions that imposed an idealist view of art.

REALISM AND FRENCH HISTORY

Realism, with its overt adherence to the representation of historical time and of things as they are, however brutal or sordid, asserted a direct challenge to the system of rules governing aesthetic conventions in France at the beginning of the nineteenth century. Realist writers were not the first to oppose neo-classicism, however. An earlier generation of Romantic writers outraged public opinion and the *Académie* in the 1820s and 1830s. Most notable of these was the poet, novelist and dramatist, Victor Hugo (1802–85). The preface to his play *Cromwell* (1827) became, in effect, the manifesto of the French Romantic movement. French romaniticism evokes a heroic world of titanic struggle and rebellion against injustice but it also elaborates a sense of the writer as a visionary in quest of non-material ideals. This theme of rejecting the world for art was a formative influence on the art for art's sake movement that developed more fully in France in the 1850s. If realist writers had perforce to position themselves in opposition to idealism as upheld by the *Académie*, they established a more complex relationship to romaniticism. Early realist writers, like Stendhal (1783–1842) and Balzac, stressed the more prosaic professionalism of the novelist rather than the writer's role as visionary. Instead of the transcendental truth of idealism, French realists espoused the new authority of science with its disciplined observation of empirical reality. Yet realist writers were in sympathy with romantic writers' rejection of classical decorum and their attitude of rebellion towards state authority and bourgeois materialism and respectability.

What is difficult for us now to grasp imaginatively is the intense politicisation of every aspect of French culture throughout its continually turbulent history for most of the nineteenth century. The storming of the Bastille in 1789 was hailed by progressives in France and elsewhere, especially in England, as symbolising the beginning of a new era. The absolutist powers of the Monarchy and Church, twin pillars of the *ancien régime*, were to be swept away and the restrictive mental horizons of superstition and servility replaced by the Enlightenment ideals of rational democracy. Yet the new Republic lasted only until 1804 when Napoleon crowned himself Emperor and led French armies triumphantly against the massed forces of European political reaction. The ideals of the Revolution became etched in the sacrifices and glories of Napoleon's armies, raised largely by mass conscription that left no family in France untouched. Napoleon's defeat by the European powers in 1815 brought the restoration of the Bourbon monarchy.

In the following decades, French national life was dominated by violent power struggles between monarchists and republicans, traditionalists and economic modernisers. In 1830, an insurrection in Paris ousted the unpopular Bourbon, Charles X. Louis-Philippe, a distant Bourbon, came to the throne on the promise of popular monarchy. He inculcated favour with the new wealthy middle class by initiating state support for railway companies and infrastructure, expansion of industry and the establishment of the Bourse as the financial exchange to promote speculative capitalism. Known as the bourgeois monarchy, the regime was bitterly denounced by both republicans and traditionalists as betraying the glory of France for the franc. Heroism and noble sacrifice had given way, it seemed, to opulent respectability. In 1848 political discontent erupted into violent protest, the king fled the capital, and a Provisional

Government of republican politicians, writers and journalists was proclaimed. The Provisional Government hastily passed progressive measures like universal male suffrage and press liberties, and a proliferation of new journals, newspapers and clubs were founded in Paris and the provinces. Yet the new Republic faced economic catastrophe at home and reactionary hostility abroad. A conservative backlash in France allowed the nephew of Napoleon, auspiciously called Louis-Napoleon Bonaparte, and his 'party of order' to seize power. After a short, harshly repressed resistance by republicans, Louis-Napoleon Bonaparte became Napoleon III in 1852. The brief Second Republic gave way to the Second Empire which was to last until 1871. (See Tombs 1996 for a clear account of the period; also Hobsbawm 1975a and 1975b; also Marx [1852] 1954 for his classic account of the *coup d'état* that established the second empire.)

French literary realism developed during the years of these political struggles and it is unsurprising that the writing is characterised by a complex consciousness of the multiple interactions of historical processes and forces upon the lives of individuals. The literary field in which realist novelists took up their positions as writers was thoroughly inter-penetrated by the partisan struggles of conflicting political affiliations. The insecurity of each new political regime ensured that censorship remained an active weapon against dissension, while the patronage of the court was extravagantly lavished on those writers who supported authority. Challenges to the consecrated literary values of classical decorum of style and language were inevitably perceived as attacks upon the dignity of the state. In such a context, French writers and artists generally could not fail to be highly aware of the formal and stylistic aspects of their work because aesthetics always carried a political dimension.

For this reason, an account of French literary realism in the nineteenth century has to keep two intertwined but separate threads in view: there is the history of the public claims, artistic manifestos and controversies in which the writers engaged, but there is also the history of their writerly practices and achievements. The two do not always map neatly one on to the other. In addition, there is also the twentieth-century critical tradition that has evaluated nineteenth-century realism as a literary form and that critical history also has its conflicts and polemics. While aiming to keep both the contemporary and the later critical debates in view, I shall give most prominence, in my account, to what I see as the artistic achievements of French nineteenth-century realist writing as practised by the major novelists of the period: Stendhal, Balzac, Flaubert, and Zola. The four defining features of this body of writing are: i) an emphasis on the particular at the expense of universal truth: the focus is upon individual characters perceived as the location of the multiple social forces and contradictions of their era; ii) formal experimentation, especially in terms of narrative perspective and linguistic innovation; iii) the novel form is a participant in the move-ment towards greater democracy and social justice; but, iv) it is also caught up and shaped by the complex tensions between the commercial demands of a mass market and the requirements of artistic integrity.

COUNT FREDERIC DE STENDHAL (1783–1842)

Stendhal, born Henri Beyle, is the earliest of the major French nine-teenth-century realists, although his influence as a writer began to develop only at the end of his life after a warm review of his last novel, *The Charterhouse of Parma* (1839), by his younger and already famous contemporary, Honoré de Balzac. Although Stendhal wrote his novels well before 'realism' became a widely used term in the mid-century aes-thetic struggles in France, his work exemplifies the defining qualities of the genre: historical particularity and stylistic innovation put to the ser-vice of sceptical secularism that ironises all idealist claims. Like many other realists, Stendhal came to novel-writing by way of journalism; he inaugurated the novelistic technique of incorporating actual items from newspapers into the texture of his fiction. He retained the journalistic practice of improvisation and rapidity, making very few revisions or cor-rections to his first drafts. Even Balzac, himself a prolific writer, criti-cised Stendhal for his apparent lack of artistic concern with style. Yet Georg Lukács sees Stendhal's frugal, disciplined prose and his rejection of romantic embellishment as one of the artistic strengths of early real-ism that would be sacrificed in later formalist developments of the genre under Flaubert (Lukács [1950] 1972: 76–7). Stendhal located his values solely in eighteenth-century rational enlightenment but he fought for fifteen years in Napoleon's Grand Army and said of the Emperor, 'he was our sole religion' (Martineau, ed., *Memoires sur*

Napoleon, quoted in Levin 1963: 86). He felt only a mocking contempt for the social values of Restoration France. The artistic position from which he represented his contemporary world was one of sceptical irony as to its pretensions and projected version of reality. Documentary precision was thus not the goal of his realist mode and, despite the particularity of detail and use of newspaper items, his fiction is full of factual inaccuracies. Nevertheless, most historians of realism agree that Stendhal was the first writer to consistently understand and represent character as the shifting location of multiple social forces. In *Mimesis*, Erich Auerbach associates Stendhal's new historical understanding of character with the immensely disturbed times in which he actively participated. Auerbach concludes that, 'Insofar as the serious realism of modern times cannot represent man otherwise than embedded in a total reality, political, social, and economic, which is concrete and constantly evolving, – as is the case today in any novel or film – Stendhal is its founder' (Auerbach [1946] 1953: 463).

Typically, the aspiring young heroes, Julien Sorel of *Scarlet and Black* (1830) and Fabrizio of *The Charterhouse of Parma*, can only be understood as coming of that generation born amid the fading glory of Napoleon's Empire and growing up to consciousness of self in the disillusionment and reactionary politics of the Restoration. Their characters and their lives are compounded of a youthful romantic idealism that gives way to disenchanted pragmatism, even cynicism. Yet ultimately they resist personal corruption. Although both Julien and Fabrizio are intensely particularised individual psychologies they can also be seen as embodying, in the typicality of their characters and in the courses that their lives take, the historical forces of an era.

Fabrizio's earliest life is suffused with the afterglow of Napoleon's liberation of Italy from the reactionary German Empire in 1796 'at the head of that youthful army which but a short time before had crossed the Bridge of Lodi, and taught the world that after so many centuries Caesar and Alexander had a successor' (Stendhal [1839] 1958: 19). Alternating with this world of largely imagined heroism and high ideals is the repressive authoritarianism of the *ancien régime* represented by Fabrizio's austere father, a man of 'boundless hatred for the new ideas' (Stendhal [1839] 1958: 27). Not surprisingly, when Fabrizio learns that Napoleon has escaped imprisonment and landed in France, he declaims fervently 'I will go forth to conquer or to die beside that Man of Destiny' (Stendhal [1839] 1958: 44). Fabrizio achieves neither of these ambitions but Stendhal's rigorously realist representation of the Battle of Waterloo has exerted a pervasive influence on subsequent artistic treatment of warfare. In this extract, Fabrizio, desperately trying to find the scene of active fighting, is befriended by a kindly *cantinière*:

'But, good Lord, I bet you don't even know how to bite open a cartridge.'

Fabrizio, though stung to the quick, admitted all the same to his new friend that she had guessed rightly.

'The poor lad! He'll be killed straight off, and that's God's truth; it won't take long. You really must come with me,' went on the *cantinière* in a tone of authority.

'But I want to fight.'

'And you shall fight too; [...] there's fighting enough today for everyone.' [...]

Fabrizio had not gone five hundred paces when his nag stopped short. It was a corpse, lying across the path, which terrified horse and rider alike.

Fabrizio's face, which was naturally very pale, took on a very decidedly greenish tinge. The *cantinière* [...] raising her eyes to look at our hero, she burst out laughing.

'Aha, my boy!' she cried, 'There's a titbit for you!' Fabrizio remained as if petrified by horror. What struck him most was the dirtiness of the feet of this corpse which had already been stripped of its shoes and left with nothing but a miserable pair of trousers all stained with blood.

'Come nearer,' said the *cantinière*, 'get off your horse, you'll have to get used to such things. Look,' she cried, 'he's got it in the head.'

A bullet, entering on one side of the nose, had come out by the opposite temple, and disfigured the corpse in a hideous fashion, leaving it with one eye still open.

'Get off your horse then, lad,' said the *cantinière*, 'and give him a shake of the hand, and see if he'll return it.'

Without hesitating, although almost ready to give up the ghost from disgust, Fabrizio flung himself off his horse and taking the hand

of the corpse gave it a vigorous shake. Then he stood still as though
no life was left in him. He did not feel he had the strength to mount
his horse again. What most particularly horrified him was the still
open eye.

(Stendhal [1839] 1958: 53–4)

As this first intimation warns, the glorious battle that Fabrizio passionately desires to join turns out to be an unheroic, brutal, chaotic, apparently purposeless series of inconclusive incidents. Following this
episode, Fabrizio fails to find any opportunity for heroic figuring, he is
snubbed and robbed by the hard-bitten regular soldiers and, most comically, he wholly fails to recognise the Emperor when he passes close by.
At the crisis of the battle he falls asleep from fatigue. The whole thrust
of Stendhal's writing is anti-idealist and anti-romantic. As in this passage, the mode of ironic mockery encompasses the hero, but events are
largely conveyed from Fabrizio's perspective so that, while his idealism is
the subject of comic deflation, there remains a sympathetic insight that
his mistakes derive from finer impulses than the self-interest and opportunism that surrounds him. We might also note Stendhal's representation of the shrewd *cantinière* who takes Fabrizio under her wing. In
most earlier forms of writing, certainly in any literature influenced by a
classical notion of decorum, she would have figured as a comic yokel. In
Stendhal's story she stands out as one of the few purposeful, resourceful
and intelligent characters. There is a democratic impulse here that influences Brecht in his choice of heroine for his play *Mother Courage*
(1941). In his epic novel *War and Peace* (1863–9) Tolstoy also drew
upon Stendhal's anti-heroic techniques.

Harry Levin claims that Stendhal's writing is characterised by an
'unremitting sense of modernity' (Levin 1963: 85). This modernity
derives largely from the pervasive secularism that constitutes Stendhal's
artistic position, producing a novelistic prose of sparse, concentrated
directness and an innovative, complex use of narrative perspective. It is
a perspective that eschews authority or claims of consecrated vision.
Typically, in his novels, the focalisation rejects traditional omniscience,
drawing the reader into the consciousness and viewpoint of the characters, especially that of the hero, while maintaining enough ironic distance to balance sympathy with a very modern sense of comic deflation.

The narrative voice sustains an intimacy of tone that interpellates the reader into a non-hierarchic, democratic familiarity with the narrator and the represented world. These are the modern, secular novelistic qualities that Stendhal offers subsequent generations of writers.

HONORÉ DE BALZAC (1799–1850)

It was the younger writer, Balzac, who made the most immediate impact upon his contemporaries and literary successors. Harry Levin states a critical consensus when he says that 'Balzac occupies the central position in any considered account of realism' (Levin 1963: 151). In the first place there is the sheer scale of his work: between 1830 and his death in 1850 he wrote about ninety novels and shorter stories involving more than two thousand characters. His days were ordered like a monastic regime in which he laboured twelve to eighteen hours out of the twenty-four on his current book. Henry James, in an affectionate essay, conveys the impact of Balzac's creative energy on a subsequent fellow writer:

> The impression then, confirmed and brightened, is of the mass and weight of the figure and of the extent of ground it occupies; a tract on which we might all of us together quite pitch our little tents, open our little booths, deal in our little wares,…I seem to see him in such an image moving about as Gulliver among the pigmies.
>
> (James 1914: 87)

Only when a large part of his great output was already published did Balzac explicitly formulate the ambitious programme he had set himself in his life's work. In 1842 he wrote the Preface [*Avant-propos*] to *The Human Comedy*, the general title he had given 'to a labour which I undertook nearly thirteen years ago' (Balzac [1842] 1981: 134). In outlining this vast project, Balzac associates the role of the writer with that of the rational scientific observer. In particular, Balzac singled out the work of Saint-Hilaire who had demonstrated that the variety of external forms distinguishing different species were the result of the environmental determinants within which each type developed. From this Balzac concluded, 'I saw that in this sense Society resembled Nature.

For does not Society make man, according to the milieux in which he acts, into as many different men as there are varieties in zoology?' (Balzac [1842] 1981: 135). Balzac was the first to use the word 'milieu' in this way but thereafter it became a central concept within French critical and sociological discourse. His task as he set it out in *The Human Comedy* was to encompass 'men, women and things, i.e. people and the material form they give their thinking' (Balzac [1842] 1981: 136). In line with his scientific paradigm of knowledge, Balzac saw himself as the 'secretary' of French Society which was itself the historian. Balzac planned to draw up an 'inventory' of the vices, virtues, passions, events and types that constitute society as a whole and in so doing 'with much patience and courage I would write the book for nineteenth-century France' (Balzac [1842] 1981: 137–8).

The scientific language and models that Balzac draws upon in parts of the 'Preface' declare his affiliation with the rational-empirical tradition stemming from eighteenth-century Enlightenment. The 'Preface' to *The Human Comedy* became, in effect, the manifesto of realism just as Hugo's 'Preface' to *Cromwell* became the central document of French romaniticism. Harry Levin argues that in writing it, Balzac inaugurated a shift in artistic values: traditional emphasis on the visionary, universalising imagination was replaced by trust in the power of scientific, objective observation. Nevertheless, the 'Preface' articulates the duality of Balzac's artistic and political allegiances. Like a good scientist, the writer should 'study the *causes or central cause* of these social facts, and discover the meaning hidden in that immense assembly of faces, passions and events' (Balzac [1842] 1981: 138). Yet the novelist whom Balzac commends for conveying the forces and energies that drive human passions and social conflicts is the romantic writer, Sir Walter Scott (1771–1832), whose characters 'are drawn up from the depth of their century' (Balzac [1842] 1981: 137). This element of romaniticism in Balzac's artistic affiliations is aligned with his political adherence to Catholicism and Monarchy, as 'eternal Truths' (Balzac [1842] 1981: 139).

Yet Balzac was a romantic royalist writing in the era of the bourgeois king, Louis-Philippe, who came to power by aligning the throne to the new force of emergent capitalism and to the new moneyed-class of financiers and industrialists. The novels that compose *The Human Comedy* constitute Balzac's perception of French history from 1789 to

1848. It is a tribute to his realist historical consciousness that, as Georg Lukács says, 'He recognized with greater clarity than any of his literary contemporaries the profound contradiction between the attempts at feudal-absolutist Restoration and the growing forces of capitalism' (Lukács [1937] 1969: 96). Despite his political and religious sympathies, Balzac's novels persistently pay tribute to the heroic nobility of the generation who risked their lives for republican ideals alongside Napoleon. Just as honestly, his fiction recognises that feudal values of reverence and homage, on which the 'eternal Truths' of monarchy and religion rest, cannot survive in a predatory world dominated by money markets.

Stendhal's fiction brought to realism an understanding of character in terms of the determining effect on individual lives of multiple capillary currents of historical change. What is additionally new and distinctive in Balzac's work is the compendious detail in which he grasps a historical milieu. Balzac, more than any other writer, developed the pictorial quality of realism. Yet this visual element is not aiming simply at photographic mimetic effect; Balzac sees his world in an intensely historical way. Erich Auerbach comments on the absolute precision with which he defines the social and historical setting of each of his characters, noting that 'to him every milieu becomes a moral and physical atmosphere which impregnates the landscape, the dwelling, furniture, implements, clothing, physique, character, surroundings, ideas, activities, and fates of men, and at the same time the general historical situation reappears as a total atmosphere which envelops all its several milieu' (Auerbach [1946] 1953: 473). What Balzac's writing forces upon our attention is the clotted thingness that constitutes modern social space. And for Balzac every thing declares its money value. As Henry James noted wryly, ' "Things" for him are francs and centimes more than any others, and I give up as inscrutable, and unfathomable, the nature, the peculiar avidity of his interest in them' (James 1914: 87). Balzac's continuous concern with money is not that surprising: he began writing the novels that form *The Human Comedy* under the immediate pressure of bankruptcy and throughout his life he remained financially insecure.

As with the pictorial effect, Balzac's practice, in his novels, of pricing and cataloguing the world of things does not aim at merely documentary accuracy. Balzac's experience of the insecurities that typified the new speculative capitalism of Louis-Philippe's France brought to his fiction a dominating sense of the rapacious energies of early venture finance. More than any other writer, Balzac insists that money is the stuff of life. For Balzac all human passions have an exact price in francs: sexual desire, family affections, noble aspiration, religious devotion, social ambition, courage, loyalty, hatred and revenge: he costs them all. In his novel, *Cousin Bette* (1846), a character comments casually, 'All one can do is to snatch as much hay as one can from the hayrack. That's what life amounts to in Paris.' In agreeing, her companion notes, 'In Paris most kindnesses are just investments' (Balzac [1846] 1965: 113, 115). Balzac's modernity as a writer consists largely in the sense, conveyed in his major fiction, of social reality as a glittering, unstable surface, a veneer that fails to mask the circulating, impersonal force of money.

From Marx and Engels onwards, realism has held a privileged position within Marxist literary criticism. This critical tradition was most fully developed by György Lukács in his two studies, *The Historical Novel* (1937) and *Studies in European Realism* (1950) Lukács acclaimed Balzac's fiction as the culminating point of realist achievement in France, emphasising two central qualities that defined this triumph of form: Balzac's ability to convey the forces of history underlying the social details of milieu and his representation of characters as types rather than as averages. In *Studies in European Realism*, Lukács claims:

> The central category and criterion of realist literature is the type, a peculiar synthesis which organically binds together the general and the particular both in characters and in situations. What makes a type a type is not its average quality,...what makes it a type is that in it all the humanly and socially essential determinants are present on their highest level of development, in the ultimate unfolding of the possibilities latent in them, in extreme presentation of their extremes, rendering concrete the peaks and limits of men and epochs.
>
> (Lukács [1950] 1972: 6)

Balzac himself seems to be saying something rather similar about his characters when he describes his method as 'individualizing the type and typifying the individual' (Souverain, *Lettres à l'Etrangère*, quoted in

Levin 1963: 200). Balzac's characters are certainly not average or 'photographic'. They are frequently monstrous, driven by obsessive passions. Balzac may see his role as being the secretary of society but his novels are peopled by figures that owe more to dreams and nightmares than to scientific categorisation. While the influence of romantic drama is clear in the heightened force of these representations, it is romaniticism brought into the service of realism. The consuming passions of his main protagonists are always tracked back in the narrative to precise historical events and contradictory social pressures so that, in their larger-than life-intensity, individual characters become demonic embodiments of impersonal historical forces. In *Cousin Bette* one of the central characters, Madame Valerie Marneffe, brings about the ruin of two very different men ostensibly by the same means: besotted lust. Yet the origin of their obsession for her is traced to very different social causes. Monsieur Crevel is one of the new men of the 1830s, a 'wealthy, self-made, retired shop-keeper' whose self-satisfied complacency marks him out as 'one of the Paris elect'; Crevel hankers after a mistress who, as a 'real lady', can set the gloss of class distinction upon his bourgeois social aspirations (Balzac [1846] 1965: 11, 131). His rival, Baron Hulot, belongs to the generation that served under Napoleon and owes his fortune (now fast-declining) to financial opportunities afforded by his attachment to the Emperor. Hulot's lechery is a desperate and pathetic search for the lost valour and glamour of his youth under the Empire. So the comically calamitous struggle of two ageing men for sexual favours enacts as farce the historical forces that brought to dominance the bourgeois regime of Louis-Philippe.

GUSTAVE FLAUBERT (1821–1880) AND THE *'RÉALISME'* CONTROVERSY IN FRANCE

For all historians of literary realism, Balzac is a central and commanding figure. Yet the term 'realism' and the controversies surrounding it did not become current in France until the mid-1850s, five years after his death. It was not a novelist but the painter, Gustave Courbet (1819–1877), who sparked off the controversy that publicised the term realism almost as a slogan. In 1855, his paintings were excluded from the Paris exhibition because of their unclassical rendering of peasants and labourers. In response, Courbet set up his own exhibition under the title *Pavillon du Réalisme*. Writers and journalists quickly rallied in defence of the kind of art that the title seemed to proclaim. Typical of the polemical tone of the times was an article by Fernand Desnoyers entitled 'Du Réalisme', which appeared in *L'Artiste* on 9 December 1855. The article begins:

> This article is neither a defence of a client nor a plea for an individual; it is a manifesto, a profession of faith. Like a grammar or a course in mathematics, it begins with a definition: Realism is the true depiction of objects.
>
> (reprinted in Becker 1963: 80.)

The article goes on to oppose realism to both classical and romantic idealisation and to over-conventionalised form: 'The writer who can depict men and things only by the aid of known and conventional means is not a realist writer' (Becker 1963: 81). From 1856 to 1857, seven monthly numbers of a magazine, *Réalisme*, kept the word and the issue before the attention of the art-conscious public. But the widest publicity and notoriety came with the trial of Flaubert's novel, *Madame Bovary*, published in 1857. The prosecution for offence to public morals was initiated by the repressive regime of Emperor Napoleon III, as the 'party of order', in an attempt to consolidate its conservative ethos of moral conformity. The trial failed but Flaubert was infuriated that his lawyers defended his book on the grounds of its edifying morality.

The acquittal of the novel was hailed as the vindication and triumph of realism yet Flaubert was reluctant to assume the title. Late in his life he wrote, 'But note that I hate what is conventionally called *realism*, although people regard me as one of its high priests' (in Becker 1963: 96). In *Madame Bovary*, Flaubert brings a poetic sensibility into a very taut balance with what he believed was required for great art: the meticulous, impersonal objectivity of the scientist. Flaubert's characters, no less than those of Balzac and Stendhal are conceived historically. Their personalities and the events of their lives are wholly shaped by the larger social forces in which their existences are enmeshed. Flaubert brings two new qualities to realist writing: his passionate commitment to artistic objectivity and his almost mystical sense of artistic dedication. There are innovative strengths but also limitations associated with both qualities.

Flaubert declared, 'It is one of my principles that you must not *write yourself.* The artist ought to be like God in creation, invisible and omnipotent. He should be felt everywhere but not seen' (in Becker 1963: 94). In *Madame Bovary* he felt he had achieved this total invisibility of the writer's own personality. Emma Bovary is a young woman whose consciousness and existence is confined to a provincial petit bourgeois milieu. Her dreams of something more gracious and impassioned in her life have been shaped wholly by romantic fiction and so her vague aspirations take the form of social elevation and romantic love. The means by which Flaubert represents her rather common-place tragedy encapsulates his main innovations to realist form. He brings a disciplined poetic intensity to subject matter that is ostensibly trivial and vulgar. He also develops a complex limitation of narrative perspective to a character's point of view, matching this by modulating his style to evoke the rhythm and tone of that person's thoughts and feelings. In the following passage Emma Bovary, passing a tedious Sunday winter afternoon on an uninteresting walk to 'a large piece of waste ground', is confronted by the contrasting appearances of her dull husband, Charles, and a younger man of their acquaintance.

> She turned round; there stood Charles, his cap pulled down over his eyes, his thick lips trembling, which lent an added stupidity to his face. Even his back, that stolid back of his, was irritating to see. His frock-coat seemed to wear upon it the whole drabness of the personality within.
>
> As she surveyed him, tasting a kind of vicious ecstasy in her irritation, Leon moved a step forward. White with cold, his face seemed to assume a softer languor; between his neck and cravat the collar of his shirt was loose and showed some skin; the tip of his ear stuck out beneath a lock of hair, and his big blue eyes, raised to the clouds, looked to Emma more limpid and more lovely than mountain tarns that mirror the sky. [...]
>
> Madam Bovary did not accompany Charles to their neighbours' that evening. [...] As she lay in bed watching the fire burn bright, the scene came back to her: Leon standing there, bending his walking-cane

in one hand, and with the other holding [the neighbour's child] Athalie, who had been calmly sucking a lump of ice. She found him charming; couldn't stop thinking of him; remembered how he had looked on other occasions, the things he had said, the sound of his voice, everything about him. And pouting out her lips as though for a kiss, she said over and over again:

'Charming, yes charming!...And in love?' she asked herself. 'In love with whom?...With me!'

(Flaubert [1857] 1950: 114–15)

Much of the writing in this passage is highly pictorial. Yet in contrast to Balzac's plethora of things, the effect is achieved here by a rigorous poetic selection of only the most telling detail: Charles's way of wearing his cap, his thick lips, the contrasting delicate tip of Leon's ear. This kind of artistic compression is the result of Flaubert's painstaking, anguished composition, often writing only a few lines a day. The perspective throughout most of the passage is that of Emma Bovary and we see the two men entirely through her eyes; the judgements are hers not the narrator's. Neither does the narrative appear to assume any evaluative attitude towards Emma, and again this contrasts with Balzac's frequent authorial commentary to explain and moralise upon his characters for the reader. Yet, although the author remains, as Flaubert says, invisible, the perspective conveyed is subtly larger and more discriminating than Emma Bovary's view of things. The writing conveys the scene that she sees but it also sees her within that scene with an objectivity she never achieves in the course of her story. Emma sees herself fantastically as a romantic heroine 'pouting her lips as though for a kiss' but the reader sees her posing as a self-imagined heroine in a romance. With similar effect, words in the passage take on the synthetic texture of Emma's own thoughts as Leon's blue eyes look to her 'more limpid and more lovely than mountain tarns that mirror the sky'. Such language points beyond Emma's own consciousness to the popular sentimental poetry and novels that are the sources of her imagining.

This shuttling narrative effect, that takes us into the shallow limitations of the heroine's individual sensibility and beyond this restriction to the determining horizons of her social milieu, sustains the pervasive ironic position from which the provincial world of *Madame Bovary* is surveyed. Nevertheless this scrupulous narrative distance does not wholly preclude reader sympathy for Emma. This is perhaps what Flaubert was getting at when he wrote, 'If *Bovary* is worth anything, it won't lack heart. Irony, however, seems to dominate life. Is this why, when I was weeping, I often used to go and look at myself in the mirror? This tendency to look down upon oneself from above is perhaps the source of all virtue' (in Becker 1963: 91). It is this ironic, detached realism that Flaubert's characters singularly fail to achieve.

The distanced poise of Flaubert's prose suggests a cultivated sensibility shared by the writer and the **implied reader**, but cannot in any way be identified with the characters in the work. Flaubert's sense of the artist's absolute dedication to his art was hugely influential in raising the status of the novel in the second half of the century but at the price of its comprehensive appeal. Balzac's financial situation absolutely required him to reach a wide readership, whereas Flaubert's independent means supported the low sales of his novels. Flaubert was one of a group of artists, including the poet Charles Baudelaire, who, by the mid-century, were proclaiming the 'disinterestedness' of art. In many ways their public pose of indifference to political and social issues derived from the political situation they found themselves in after 1852. (Bourdieu 1996: 107–112 provides a detailed analysis of the historical development of aesthetic claims for artistic disinterestedness in mid to late nineteenth-century France.) Republicanism and revolution failed in 1848 and the Second Empire, that crushed radical political hopes, was a travesty of the ideals that had brought the first Empire into existence under Napoleon. For many writers after 1852 the only integrity that seemed available was the disinterested pursuit of art for art's sake and a disdainful contempt for the bourgeois values that had brought Louis-Napoleon to power as Napoleon III.

One effect of this disaffection was an increasing tendency for serious artists to address themselves to a small select audience of the like-minded. The romantic writers of the 1830s had first represented the poet-artist as an alienated figure at odds with a corrupted society. By the end of the 1850s, the sense of aloof separation from bourgeois philistinism and materialistic self-serving had become the prevalent attitude among many artists in France. This artistic contempt for their public was dramatically expressed in the Preface that Edmond and Jules de

Goncourt, prominent members of the Flaubert circle, wrote for their novel *Germinie Lacerteux* (1864):

> The public likes false novels: this is a true novel....
> The public further likes innocuous and consoling reading, adventures which end happily, imaginings which upset neither its digestion nor its serenity: this book with its sad and violent distraction, is so made as to go against its habits and be injurious to its hygiene.
>
> (Auerbach [1946] 1953: 494–5)

The striking identity between this language and some of the language encountered in the critique of realism outlined in Part I indicates the bridging point of the two chronologies. Modernism and postmodernism inherit from the *l'art pour l'art* movement of the French mid-century not only a radical concern with formal experimentation but also the more questionable ideology of 'cultivation' as an aloof sensibility that keeps its distance from the vulgarity of mass culture.

Lukács argues that this disengagement by Flaubert and his generation from active participation in the social conflicts of their era brought the dynamic vitality of the realist tradition to an end in France (Lukács [1937] 1969: 246–7). For all his artistic perfection, Flaubert is a lesser writer than Balzac, Lukács argues, because he diverts the writer's proper concern to evoke the immense historical forces determining social reality into the pursuit of style. Moreover, Flaubert's aim of total scientific objectivity encompasses only what is average, failing to grasp the importance of Stendhal's and Balzac's representation of the individual character as historical type. Lukács concludes that because Flaubert lacks Balzac's conception of the organic relationship between an individual and the social moment that conditions their existence, his representation is limited to personal psychology (Lukács [1937] 1969: 224).

Most critics recognise Flaubert as a pivotal figure in French literature. His poeticisation of the language of prose was important for the *Symboliste* movement in France in the 1880s which was a reaction against the publicised scientific aims of realism, particularly as insisted upon by the powerful French critic Hippolyte Taine (1828–93). *Symbolisme* was in turn a formative influence upon French and British literary modernism. Yet most critics also count Flaubert's novels among the high achievements of French realism. Erich Auerbach sums up more positively than Lukács, Flaubert's dual artistic position that straddles a realist commitment to the social world and an idealist dedication to aesthetic disinterestedness:

> Flaubert may insist that he is an artist and nothing but an artist. The more one studies Flaubert, the clearer it becomes how much insight into the problematic nature and the hollowness of nineteenth-century bourgeois culture is contained in his realist works....the political, economic and social subsoil appears comparatively stable and at the same time intolerably charged with tension'.
>
> (Auerbach [1946] 1953: 490–1)

Realist form, throughout the nineteenth century, continually revises itself. Flaubert could not write like Balzac because he did not live in the same reality. What he undoubtedly established was the status of the realist novel as a form of art, he extended the democratic reach of the genre by the serious and sympathetic treatment of average people, like Emma Bovary who had previously not figured in literary traditions, and he developed, further than Stendhal, the complex artistic potential of narrative technique.

ÉMILE ZOLA (1840–1902)

Zola was twenty years younger than Flaubert. The literary field in which he had to make a position for himself was completely different from that in which Balzac had achieved fame and quite different from that which had confronted Flaubert. Two processes in particular are important for an understanding of Zola's literary realism. In 1859 Charles Darwin published *On the Origin of Species* and theories of natural selection were quickly popularised, seeming to underwrite the authority of a scientific model of knowledge. Second, by the last decades of the century, the practice of literature was completely absorbed into the commercial market place. In the struggle for sales, publicity, even notoriety, became a key factor. Unlike Flaubert, Zola depended for his livelihood on the success of his novels. His determination to impose himself on the literary world is characterised by a commercial opportunism that is inseparable from his serious artistic commitment.

Zola recognised that, in the commercialised literary field of late nineteenth-century France, a slogan and a manifesto were effective means of self-publicity. The slogan he chose was 'Naturalism' and he set out his claims for this, and for his own work, in *The Experimental Novel* (1880). During the 1860s and 1870s, the influential French historian and literary critic Hippolyte Taine had vigorously expounded a determinist view of reality, expanding Balzac's notion of milieu as the means by which literary art could incorporate the documentary methodology of natural sciences. Responding to the influence of Taine as well as Darwin, Zola pushed Balzac's and Flaubert's espousal of science to the logical extreme. In *The Experimental Novel*, he advocated 'the idea of literature determined by science', taking as his explicit model the work of Dr Claude Bernard in *Introduction à l'Etude de la Médicine Expérimental* (reprinted in Becker 1963: 162). Using the experimental method developed by scientists and doctors, Zola argues, novelists, too, can produce new knowledge of the passionate and intellectual life of human beings which is their special provenance. Following Claude Bernard, Zola describes experiment as provoked observation. 'The novelist,' he continues, 'is both an observer and an experimenter. The observer in him presents the data as he has observed them,…Then the experimenter appears and institutes the experiment, that is, sets the characters of a particular story in motion in order to show that the series of events therein will be those demanded by the determinism of the phenomena under study' (Becker 1963: 166). As this last sentence suggests, Zola accepts a Darwinian sense of the determining power of environment and heredity on all living organisms. The experimental novel, therefore, aims to show 'the influences of heredity and surrounding circumstances, then to show man living in the social milieu which he himself has produced, which he modifies every day, and in the midst of which he in his turn undergoes continuous modification,…and [by this method] to resolve scientifically the question of knowing how men behave themselves once they are in society' (Becker 1963: 174). Zola counters the claim that, in following this experimental model, the naturalist novelist denies the importance of artistic imagination. Naturalist novelists are certainly concerned to start from a detailed knowledge of the relevant social facts but in setting in motion the experimental plot, the writer calls upon the power of invention and that is the 'genius in the book' (Becker 1963: 168). Zola was continually attacked for what was seen as his evolutionary focus upon the sordid and bestial aspects of human existence, especially the sexual, but in *The Experimental Novel* he rejects idealism, declaring 'There is no nobility, no dignity, no beauty, no morality in not knowing,...The only great and moral works are true works' (Becker 1963: 184).

It is only too easy to spot the fallacy in Zola's claim that the novelist's own plot can function as a scientific verification of the laws of heredity. It is more generally Zola's detractors that have held him accountable to his naturalist manifesto. Zola himself seems to have admitted that he adopted the label 'naturalism' with a view to publicity: 'I repeated it over and over because things need to be baptized, so that the public will regard them as new' (quoted in Levin 1963: 305). Zola's great series of twenty novels, *Les Rougon-Macquart*, claiming to show the slow evolutionary workings of heredity and environment through the history of one extended family, was already half-completed before he explicitly formulated his notions of the experimental method. Yet this should not be taken to indicate that Zola was not seriously committed to the pursuit of a materialist, scientific view of reality and Harry Levin is surely correct when he says that 'no comparable man of letters...tried so hard to grasp the scientific imagination' (Levin 1963: 309).

'Imagination' is the key word here; like the other major French realists, Zola the 'naturalist' is also a poet and romanticist. Those parts of his novels that least convince are the passages that baldly state a mechanical view of hereditary or environmental determinism. Zola's first published piece was a fairy tale that he described as a 'poetic dream' (quoted in Levin 1963: 318). The power of his realism derives from his fusion of detailed factual observation of social reality with the visual intensity of dream or nightmare. What Zola brings to realism is the use of poetic symbolism and imagery to convey the awesome power of huge, impersonal industrial and political forces exerted on human life. The opening chapter of *Germinal* (1885) in which the out-of-work hero, Etienne Lantier, approaches the coal-mining district of northern France, a scene of bitter conflict between labour and capital, provides a powerful example of the intensity Zola achieves. In these extracts,

Etienne, frozen with cold, is drawn irresistibly to a fire at the pit-head of Le Voreux mine and into conversation with an old man employed at the surface:

> And then they both went on grousing, in short sentences as the wind caught their breath. Etienne told him about his week's useless tramping around. Had he just got to peg out with hunger then? Soon there would be nothing but beggars on the roads. Yes, the old man agreed, it was bound to end up in a row, for, by God, you couldn't throw all these decent people out on the streets. [...]
>
> The young man waived an arm at the unfathomable darkness.
>
> 'Who does all this belong to, then?'
>
> But just at that moment Bonnemort was choked by such a violent fit of coughing that he could not get his breath. At length, after spitting and wiping the black foam off his lips, he said into the howling wind:
>
> 'What? Who does this belong to? God knows....People....'
>
> And he pointed to some vague unknown distant spot in the night, where these people lived for whom the Maheus had been hacking coal at the seam for a hundred and six years. His voice had taken on a kind of religious awe, as though he were speaking of some inaccessible tabernacle, where dwelt unseen the gorged and crouching deity whom they all appeased with their flesh but whom nobody had ever seen.
>
> 'If only you could eat your fill,' said Etienne for the third time, without any obvious transition. [...]
>
> Where was there to go and what was to become of him in a land ravaged by unemployment? Was he to leave his corpse behind some wall, like a stray dog? And yet here on this naked plain, in this thick darkness, he had a feeling of hesitation; Le Voreux struck fear into him. Each squall seemed fiercer than the last, as though each time it blew from an even more distant horizon. No sign of dawn; the sky was dead: only the furnaces and coke ovens glared and reddened the shadows, but did not penetrate their mystery. And, huddled in its lair like some evil beast, Le Voreux crouched ever lower and its breath came in longer and deeper gasps, as though it were struggling to digest its meal of human flesh.
>
> (Zola [1885] 1954: 22, 27–8)

We can recognise in the characters of this novel the culminating point of the democratic impulse of realism. The people who constitute Zola's fictional world come largely from the lowest social levels and earn their living by the most gruelling and poorly paid forms of labour. He has been criticised for the way in which he represents his human figures as dwarfed by social forces, denied agency and wholly propelled by determining circumstances. Yet it is surely undeniable that much of human existence consists of such vulnerability and powerlessness. Moreover, the vigour of the characters' language and the vitality it imparts to Zola's narration ('Had he just got to peg out with hunger then?') belies the passivity imposed by economic necessity. Zola's absorption of the ordinary discourses of work, of the streets and of working-class life into his novelistic prose was seen as an offence against the purity of French literary language, but the poet Stéphane Mallarmé (1842–98) recognised it as a quite new exploration of the capacities of poetic language. By incorporating the language of the characters into narrative language, Zola also cancels the distance maintained by Flaubert whose aloof irony encompasses the circumscribed consciousness of the protagonists within its more knowing reach. In the passages above, as in Zola's work generally, the narrative perspective remains on the same level as that of the characters claiming no superior knowledge or more cultivated sensibility.

Moreover the attitude articulated by his novels in their total effect is certainly not one of fatalistic or submissive acceptance of suffering and injustice. His work, no less than his campaign on behalf of the unjustly court-marshalled and imprisoned Captain Dreyfus, is an insistent 'J'accuse' levelled at the state and at the powerful. (For an account of the Dreyfus affair, see Tombs 1996: 462–72.) Zola transformed the newly won authority based on artistic disinterestedness into a moral imperative to writers to speak out for those without a public voice: the responsibility to bear witness. Erich Auerbach praises Zola as 'one of the very few authors of the century who created their work out of the great problems of the age' (Auerbach [1946] 1953: 512). Despite his claims to scientific method and the documentary investigations of mines, of prostitution, of the working of railways and laundries that he carried out before embarking on any novel, the power of Zola's realist engagement derives from his imaginative transformation of factual detail into memorable artistic form. The image of Le Voreux gasping as it gorges on human flesh fuses mechanical knowledge of the workings of the ventilation shaft and lift into an unforgettable image of industrial capitalism's unshrinking appetite for the muscle and bone that constitutes human labour. This kind of extended symbolism is kept grounded in the particularity of the fictional world by Zola's ability to select the one telling detail out of the mass of his preparatory documentation. In the opening section of *Germinal* the unseen deity of the mine spews out as black foam on the old man's lips. Flaubert said of Zola's novel *Nana* that it 'turns into a myth without ceasing to be real' and this is equally true of all Zola's major novels (quoted in Levin 1963: 325).

THE FUTURE OF LITERARY REALISM

Given the social and political content of Zola's work, it seems somewhat puzzling that Marxist critic, Georg Lukács, should have seen him also as sharing in the decline of what he terms the classic realism of Balzac and Stendhal. For Lukács the defining achievement of classic realism was the organic perception of the human being as the location of multiple, often contradictory social forces. This fundamental insight was materialised, for Lukács, in the way both Stendhal and Balzac conceived of characters as types, at once highly individualised, even monstrous, but simultaneously as embodiments of prevailing historical energies and conflicts. For Lukács, after Balzac this comprehensive understanding of human existence was fragmented. The political alienation of writers like Flaubert and, Lukács claims, even Zola, entails a loss of insight into social forces. Zola, Lukács argues, retreated to a belief in scientific progress and the literary naturalism that he initiated projects an impoverished perception of human nature conceived almost entirely in terms of biological determinism (Lukács [1950] 1972: 86). On the other hand, Flaubert is seen by Lukács as the originator of the subjectivist novel centred upon purely individual psychology and overly concerned with artistic form. This second trend culminated for Lukács in what he terms the decadence of modernism in which **formalism** usurped artistic commitment to social reality. It was this wholesale rejection of modernism in favour of classic realism that provoked the opposing responses of Adorno and Benjamin included in Chapter 1.

The dramatist Bertholt Brecht (1898–1956) was also stung into a vigorous retort against Lukács but he did so as an advocate of realism not modernism. Brecht argues passionately that art cannot stand still. What was reality for Balzac no longer exists so 'we must not conjure up a kind of Valhalla of the enduring figures of literature' (cited in Taylor 1980: 70). Experimental art is necessary to keep pace with social transformations of everyday reality. Avant-garde art in that sense is neither empty formalism nor elitist. Brecht insisted that 'There is not only such a thing as *being popular*, there is also the process of *becoming popular*' (Taylor 1980: 85). In that sense, experimentalism, popular art and realism become allies not terms of opposition to one another. He concluded: 'If we wish to have a living and combative literature, which is fully engaged with reality and fully grasps reality, a truly popular literature, we must keep step with the rapid development of reality' (Taylor 1980: 85). The realist novels of Stendhal, Balzac, Flaubert, and Zola resulted from the combative position that all four writers, in their different ways, took to the literary and social fields that constituted their conditions of existence. As Harry Levin reminds us, during the nineteenth century:

> They were dammed by critics, ignored by professors, turned down by publishers, opposed by the academies and the Salons, and censored and suppressed by the state. Whatever creed of realism they professed, their work was regarded as a form of subversion, and all the forces of convention were arrayed against them.
>
> (Levin 1963: 72–3)

4

LITERARY REALISM IN NINETEENTH-CENTURY BRITAIN

British literary realism has a less heroic history than that of France. The literary field was not nearly so antagonistic as the French for the obvious reason that the larger field of national power politics was also less turbulent. The nineteenth century, after a period of oppressive reactionary politics in the two decades immediately following the French Revolution, saw the extension of parliamentary democracy to the middle class in the Reform Act of 1832 and to large numbers of working-class men in 1867. The growth of Empire in the last decades of the century helped to consolidate a sense of national identity that endowed even the least of Queen Victoria's subjects with a pleasing sense of inherent superiority over the rest of the world. This more evolutionary form of social and political change resulted in a literary field in Britain that was relatively less polarised and interpenetrated by wider struggles for power. What is more, the absence in Britain of any equivalent to the *Académie français* and its concern to safeguard neoclassical correctness, also made for a far less antagonistic literary context in which new writers had to establish themselves. As in France, the novel was not really recognised in Britain as a serious literary form until after the mid-century, but unlike France it had already established a firm history and tradition during the eighteenth century. Early French novelists like Stendhal and Balzac had to look to Britain for the origin of their craft.

THE EARLY DEVELOPMENT OF BRITISH LITERARY REALISM

In *The Rise of the Novel* (1987), Ian Watt traces the establishment of a realist mode of writing as it developed during the eighteenth century in the fictional works of Daniel Defoe (1660–1731), Samuel Richardson (1689–1761) and Henry Fielding (1707–54). He links this firmly to the empirical tradition of philosophy stemming from René Descartes (1596–1650) and John Locke (1632–1704), which, he says, 'begins from the position that truth can be discovered by the individual through his senses' (Watt [1957] 1987: 12). This emphasis upon the individual apprehension of reality marks a shift from the classical concern with universal truth to a notion of particularity. This particularised epistemological perspective, stemming from Locke's *Essay concerning Human Understanding* (1690), brought a new emphasis within literature upon individualised character, located in a carefully specified place and time. Watt illustrates this innovative shift to particularity by noting how proper names for characters and places in novels changed from allegorical ones, or ones suggesting essential attributes like Squire Allworthy, to more realistic ones like Moll Flanders or Elizabeth Bennett. With particularity as the artistic aim, there came a stress on verisimilitude as accuracy of detail and correspondence to external reality. Watt associates the new novel genre with the decrease of aristocratic patronage to literature during the eighteenth century, and an increase in more commercial forms of publication for the increasingly prosperous middle class. The novel came to replace the courtly form of romance, a narrative genre based upon the ideals of chivalry. In romances, idealised knights and ladies meet with fantastic adventures in enchanted landscapes, peopled by magical figures of good and evil. Courtly forms of literature required a taste educated by classical learning and cultivated leisure. Growing wealth gave the eighteenth-century bourgeoisie, especially women, more time freed from work, but the literary forms that expanded to meet that new demand were the interrelated ones of journalism and the novel. Watt emphasises the significant role played by the middle class in the development of the eighteenth-century realist novel. He also points out the importance of Defoe's heroine, Moll Flanders, and Richardson's heroine, Clarissa, in establishing the individualised psychological realism that is one of the novel genre's out-standing achievements. Yet he fails to recognise just how important women writers were to the successful rise of the novel. (Spencer 1986 redresses this balance.)

The longer, less politicised history of the development of the novel genre in Britain is an influential factor shaping a different real-ist tradition to that of France. Three other cultural differences were important. Women novelists, such as Austen, the three Brontës, Gaskell and Eliot, played a central role in the development of nine-teenth-century realism in Britain. The strong dissenting tradition within British culture fostered a scrutinising emphasis upon individ-ual consciousness but as a down-side puritanism also sustained moral conservatism. The relationship of realism to romanticism in the British novel is also different to that which developed in France. (Stone 1980 offers a scholarly account of the influence of Romantic writing upon novelists.) In the first place, while individual British novelists were variously and pervasively influenced by individual Romantics, there was, during the first half of the century, very little recognition of British Romanticism as a cohesive movement taking up clearly defined aesthetic and political positions within the literary field. (Day 1996: 84 makes this point and provides a fully histori-cized discussion of English Romantic writing.) In France, Romantic writers had spearheaded the attack upon classicism. In Britain, lack-ing the oppressive influence of an Academy, Romantic writers tended to position themselves in opposition to Jeremy Bentham's (1748–1832) rational philosophy of utilitarianism, understood as hostile to the truths of imaginative creativity and the sympathetic heart. Romantic writers like William Blake (1757–1827) and William Hazlitt (1778–1830) and later Thomas Carlyle (1795–1881) lam-basted utilitarianism as a bleak philosophy of statistical facts that was used to justify a punitive attitude to the labouring poor, codified as The New Poor Laws of 1834. This romantic critique, linking eigh-teenth-century rationality to repressive political authority, is one rea-son why realist writers, during the first half of the century at least, were wary of identifying the aims of the novelist with those of the scientist in the way that Balzac, Flaubert and Zola had done.

A DISTINCTIVE BRITISH TRADITION OF NINETEENTH-CENTURY LITERARY REALISM

These cultural differences between the two countries have the effect of making the British nineteenth-century novel less explicit as to its realist project. Humanist critic Erich Auerbach and Marxist critic György Lukács identify two defining achievements of nineteenth-century realism: first, the perception that individual lives are the location of historical forces and contradictions and second, the serious artistic treatment of ordinary people and their experience. British nineteenth-century novelists also write out of a historicised imagination but they articulate a less explicit sense of history than writers like Stendhal and Balzac. This is not surprising, given the less tumultuous national history. As in *Daniel Deronda* (1874–6), where Eliot figures the economic reality of speculative capitalism as gambling, British novelists typically represent social forces of change at deeper structural levels or by means of symbolism and imagery. The critic, Raymond Williams (1921–88), for example, argues that a major element of Dickens's innovative realism is 'to dramatize those social institutions and consequences which are not accessible to ordinary physical observation' by means of metaphor and figuration (Williams 1974: 30). Indeed, more generally, the development of writerly techniques of indirection and suggestion is a distinguishing feature of British realism. This is perhaps a creative dividend of the moral puritanism which forbade writers the direct expression of many aspects of human experience.

British novelists also participate in the democratic impulse of realism: from Jane Austen through to Thomas Hardy, fictional representation moves away from the world of the higher gentry to the working-class sphere of characters like Tess of the D'Urbervilles and Jude the Obscure. In George Eliot's *Adam Bede* (1859), when the narrator associates the art of novel-writing with the realism of Dutch paintings, she does so in the cause of sympathetically rendering 'monotonous homely existence' and the hidden value of humble life, 'old women scraping carrots with their work-worn hands' (Eliot [1859] 1980: ch. 17, 224). This passage in *Adam Bede* is one of Eliot's most explicit elaborations of her realist aims and of her rejection of idealism in art; her sense of the artist's responsibility, she says, is 'to give a faithful account of men and things as they have mirrored themselves in my mind' (Eliot [1859] 1980: 222). Yet in the very next sentence she admits the near impossibility of achieving a representation of reality that is 'faithful' in terms of the objective ideals of science. The mind as a mirror 'is doubtless defective; the outlines will sometimes be disturbed, the reflection faint and confused' (Eliot [1859] 1980: 222). Rather than rehearse again the main features of realism that British realists share with French nineteenth-century novelists, in particular, the historicised and democratic understanding of character and event, I will focus upon the more interesting difference: the sense of doubt and ambivalence at the heart of British realism.

In *The English Realist Imagination: English Fiction from Frankenstein to Lady Chatterley*, George Levine convincingly demonstrates that nineteenth-century novelists wrote from an alert awareness of 'the possibilities of indeterminate meaning' and 'the arbitrariness of the reconstructed order to which they point' (Levine 1981: 4). One of the main reasons for this uncertainty and scepticism towards any claim that novels can provide faithful or accurate representations of reality is the pervasive influence of romanticism on all of the major nineteenth-century British novelists. Ian Watt is right to emphasise the centrality of Enlightenment thought, especially the philosophy of Locke, upon the development of the eighteenth-century novel, but for nineteenth-century writers like the Brontës, Dickens, Eliot, and even Hardy that is only half the story. Their attitude to the claims of rational scientific models of knowledge is filtered through the Romantic critique of utilitarian thinking. Frequently, sympathetic imagination is regarded as a more reliable guide to aspects of reality than rational objectivity. In addition, the tradition of dissent provides an inherent tendency to question authoritative views on what constitutes social reality and an impulse to undermine dominant perspectives with opposing viewpoints. This more multiple sense of 'reality' is also fostered by a tradition of popular culture, which includes fairy tales, melodrama, poetry, religious and radical discourses. All of these forms feed into the realist novel genre, often through the medium of romanticism. For this reason, over-simple definitions of realism have difficulty in accommodating the achievements of British nineteenth-century novels. Yet, as George Levine argues, this writing 'always implies an attempt to use language to get beyond language, to discover some non-verbal truth out there' (Levine 1981: 6) and thus is properly regarded as realist. This definition is even generous enough to comprehend *Wuthering Heights* (1847), the novel that most radically draws upon romanticism, popular culture and multiple perspectives to undercut any epistemological certainty.

Wuthering Heights concentrates all of those qualities that separate the English nineteenth-century novel from the French. It is, of course, written by a woman. Unlike France, women writers made a major contribution to the development of British realism and in particular to its characteristic questioning of the nature of social realities. An influential tradition of feminist criticism has highlighted the role of female characters in nineteenth-century women's novels as subversively 'other'; mad doubles of virtuous heroines, midnight witches and monsters (Gilbert and Gubar 1979). This vein of otherness and madness undoubtedly contributes powerfully to the ambivalent and multiple sense of reality conveyed by texts like *Jane Eyre*, *Villette*, and Mary Elizabeth Braddon's (1837–1915) sensational best-seller, *Lady Audley's Secret* (1862), for example. Yet it is perhaps timely, and, in the context of realism, certainly appropriate, to recognise equally the long line of clever, rational, witty, imaginative, resilient and able women characters found in all of Austen's novels, as the protagonists of Anne Brontë's *The Tenant of Wildfell Hall* (1848), Charlotte Brontë's *Jane Eyre* (1847), *Shirley* (1849), and *Villette* (1853), as Nelly in Emily Brontë's *Wuthering Heights* (1847), and as major characters in Elizabeth Gaskell's novels *Mary Barton* (1848), *Ruth* (1853), *North and South* (1855) and *Wives and Daughters* (1866). George Eliot's heroines are undoubtedly some of the most intelligent in fiction, but the novelist who wrote so sternly on 'silly women novelists' has an unfortunate tendency of making her clever women rather silly (Pinney 1963: 300–24). The most obvious contribution that women writers make to realism by means of such characters is the extension of subject matter. The perception of reality is broadened to encompass a view of women as rational, capable, initiating and energetic. Male writers like Flaubert with *Madame Bovary* (1857) and Tolstoy with *Anna Karenina* (1875–7) have written impressive books centred upon female protagonists, but in these texts women are understood predominantly in terms of their relationships with men and as victims of patriarchal codes.

The women writers I am discussing construct plots that frequently turn upon gender relations and a love story but their perception of their female characters is not determined by these relationships. Women in their stories are intelligently complex beings, producers of distinctive knowledge of the world and highly capable of executive action.

In addition to offering a more extensive representation of the reality that constitutes the female half of the human race, women writers' representation of women also articulates a different view of the ideological division of the social world into a public sphere governed by 'masculine' rationality and a domestic sphere of affections and sensibility with women largely restricted to the latter. In Jane Austen's last novel, *Persuasion* (1818), Admiral Croft's wife puts the hero, Captain Wentworth, her brother, robustly in his place: 'But I hate to hear you talking so,…as if women were all fine ladies, instead of rational creatures. We none of us expect to be in smooth water all our days' (Austen [1818] 1990: 69). Mrs Croft goes on to recount how she has spent most of her married life on board a ship, crossing the Atlantic four times and travelling to the East Indies, 'though many women have done more' (Austen [1818] 1990: 70). She concludes that it was only on the occasion of enforced normal domesticity in Britain 'that I ever really suffered in body or mind, the only time that I ever fancied myself unwell' (Austen [1818] 1990: 70). This exchange offers a sudden sharp glimpse of a quite different reality to the one usually conveyed of nineteenth-century women: it reminds us of women as intrepid travellers and pioneers, sharing hardships and dangers alongside men throughout the century. Mrs Croft suggests that a 'feminine' domestic sensibility is not the opposite of a 'masculine' rational capacity, rather emotional sensibility is what happens to rational energies when they are denied active outlet by domestic confinement.

At the conclusion of the story, it is the heroine, Anne Elliot's, rational understanding and the initiatives she takes on the basis of it, that bring about her reconciliation with Frederick Wentworth. In this section of the novel, Austen marks his masculine discourse with indicators of emotional distress and indecision: whereas Anne's response is given as 'replied', Wentworth's is given as 'cried he' and his sentences take the form of exclamations and questions in comparison to Anne's firm statements. The heroine, indeed, gently rebukes his failure of rational judgement: 'You should have distinguished,' Anne replied. 'You should not have suspected me now; the case so different, and my age so different' (Austen [1818] 1990: 230). Wentworth is forced to admit that due to the strength of irrational feelings 'I could not derive benefit from the late knowledge I had acquired of your character' (Austen [1818] 1990: 230). In contrast, Anne affirms the rational correctness of her thinking and actions: 'I have been thinking over the past, and trying impartially to judge of the right and wrong, I mean with regard to myself; and I must believe that I was right' (Austen [1818] 1990: 232).

'I must believe that I was right' equally summarises the impressive rational capacities and principled action of Eleanor Dashwood in *Sense and Sensibility* (1811), Fanny Price in *Mansfield Park* (1814), Jane Eyre in *Jane Eyre*, Lucy Snowe in *Villette* (1853), Margaret Hale in *North and South* (1855), Molly Gibson in *Wives and Daughters* (1866), Romola in *Romola*, and Dorothea Brooke in *Middlemarch* (1871–2). Women writers further show that the crucial mechanisms of social relationships, the structures of marriage, parenthood and family life as well as the daily maintenance of domestic affairs rest upon women's production of knowledge, their rational judgement, and executive and management skills. Mrs Croft in *Persuasion* claims the right as a wife to traverse the conventional boundaries of public and private spheres. By the mid nineteenth century the protagonists of women-authored texts are represented on the point of assuming active roles within the public sphere in their own right: Lucy Snowe as a teacher running her own school, Margaret Hale as an industrial property owner and social worker among the London poor and Dorothea Brooke, albeit as a subordinate helper to her progressive MP husband.

This challenge to the conventional gendered categorization of the social world is part of a more fundamental questioning of the nature of reality. Women realist writers are particularly aware of the fictional nature of representation and the vested interests lodged in authoritative truth claims. In *Persuasion* a male character tries to refute Anne Elliot's defence of the integrity of women's attachments, asserting 'all histories are against you, all stories, prose and verse.' (Austen [1818] 1990: 220). Anne replies, 'If you please, no reference to examples in books. Men have had every advantage of us in telling their own story. Education has been theirs in so much higher a degree; the pen has been in their hands. I will not allow books to prove anything.' (Austen [1818] 1990: 221). She concludes that the different perspectives of men and women constitutes 'a difference of opinion which does not admit of proof' (Austen [1818] 1990: 221). Women writers transform this recognition that scientific objectivity is impossible into the structuring irony of their narrative technique. Women's writing articulates a comic duality, at times a disturbing multiplicity of viewpoints.

Charlotte Brontë's narrators typically cast doubt upon the conventional notion of reality entertained by the comfortably respectable. As narrator of *Villette* (1853), the character Lucy Snowe emphasises the shifting unreliability of perspective and the uncertain boundaries between actuality and hoped for or feared realities. Leaving England for Europe in search of a wider horizon of life, Lucy Snowe describes at some length the inspiring scene that she envisions from the deck of the ship as it crosses the Channel. Europe lies before her like a dream-land, bathed in sunshine, 'making the long coast one line of gold' (Brontë [1853] 2000: ch. 5, 56). The detailed description ends abruptly: 'Cancel the whole of that, if you please reader – or rather let it stand, and draw thence a moral – an alliterative, text-hand copy – "Daydreams are delusions of the demon"' (Brontë [1853] 2000: 57). There is absolutely no way of stabilising any one authentic or objective point of view from the oscillating possibilities of this passage.

In Eliot's *Middlemarch* (1871–2) the narrative perspective ironically undercuts the authority of young doctor Lydgate's new scientific enterprise and the Reverend Casaubon's traditional scholarship. Both men aspire to be extraordinary producers of knowledge, but both are shown to be damagingly defective in their egoistic perception of a single reality that suits their own interests and blinds them to the other realities that will determine their lives. In Gaskell's *Wives and Daughters* (1866), the narrative juxtaposes the scientific knowledge of Dr Gibson and evolutionary biologist Roger Hamley to the discourses of fairy tales and poetry, associated with women. Medical and biological advances depend upon the precision and acuteness with which the scientific practitioners observe natural phenomena and the intelligence with which they interpret these external signs. The comedy of the story resides in the huge blunders in perception and interpretation that both men make. In particular, their understanding of women is shown to be invested in the domain of fairy stories and sentimental poetry, while the viewpoints of the women characters are represented in the text as clear-sighted, goal-directed and knowledgeable.

There is an obvious reason for women writers to exploit the possibilities of narrative technique to suggest that what is seen as 'reality' depends on the social position of the perceiver. But this development of perspective is not confined to them. Dickens continually aims in his writing practice to dwell upon 'the romantic side of familiar things' (Dickens [1852–3] 1996: 6), as he expresses it in his preface to *Bleak House* (1852–3). Thackeray was determinedly anti-romantic and was identified as 'chief of the realist school' by *Fraser's Magazine* in 1851 (p. 86) but he too makes innovative use of apparently traditional narrators to put in question the conventional truth claims made for realist fiction. In *The Newcomes* (1853–5), the narrator playfully mocks the convention of omniscience with its assumption that past conversations and personal feelings can be faithfully represented. This scepticism is then extended to scientific narratives by means of an analogy drawn between the novelist and the evolutionary anatomist:

All this story is told by one, who, if he was not actually present at the circumstances here narrated, yet had information concerning them, and could supply such a narrative of facts and conversations as is, indeed, not less authentic than the details we have of other histories. How can I tell the feelings of a young lady's mind; the thoughts in a young man's bosom? – As Professor Owen or Professor Agassiz takes a fragment of bone, and builds an enormous forgotten monster out of it, wallowing in primeval quagmires, tearing down leaves and branches of plants that flourished thousands of years ago, and perhaps may be coal by this time – so the novelist puts this and that together: from the footprint finds the foot; the brute who trod on it; from the brute the plant he browsed on, the marsh in which he swam – and thus, in his humble way a physiologist too, depicts the habits, size, appearance of the beings whereof he has to treat; traces this slimy reptile through the mud, and describes his habits filthy and rapacious; prods down this butterfly with a pin, and depicts his beautiful coat and embroidered

> waistcoat; points out the singular structure of yonder more impor-
> tant animal, the megatherium of his history.
>
> (II, 9; Thackeray [1850] 1996: 81)

Typically, in this passage, Thackeray makes no appeal to the artist's intuition or poetic insight as the means of entering into the feelings of his characters; rather he likens the process to the rational deductions of investigative science. Paradoxically, though, under the imaginative impulse of the writing, science itself becomes the discovery of the marvellous and the monstrous. The culminating metaphoric intensification of language shifts the meaning even further from the realm of rational order, hinting at hidden psychic realities and potentially monstrous impulses lurking beneath the surface of appearances.

By a rich variety of such means, British nineteenth-century realism exploited narrative techniques to question the nature of reality, especially as it took the form of any authoritative truth. British realist writing also has a marked tendency to radically undercut what was for Locke the privileged site of knowledge: individual identity and consciousness. Despite the particularised individuality of novelistic characters in nineteenth-century British fiction, closer analysis frequently reveals that they are represented as shifting, unstable or multiple subjectivities. Dickens's work in particular, with its representation of strange states of mind and obsessive patterns of behaviour, was highly influential on later writers like Fydor Dostoevsky (1821–81) and Franz Kafka (1883–1924). In an early episode of *Oliver Twist* (1837–8), Oliver goes with Mr Sowerbury, the undertaker, to a scene of utter destitution where they have to measure for a coffin a young woman dead from starvation. Her husband and children sob bitterly but her old mother suddenly hobbles forward:

> 'She was my daughter,' said the old woman, nodding her head in the direction of the corpse; [...] 'Lord, Lord! Well it *is* strange that I who gave birth to her, and was a woman then, should be alive and merry now; and she lying there: so cold and stiff! Lord, Lord! – to think of it; – it's as good as a play – as good as a play!'.
>
> (Dickens 1982: ch. 5, 32)

This is a dramatic example of how fairy tales and popular culture, especially popular theatre, feed into Dickens's work to produce some of its most powerful and disturbing effects. The mad old woman's grotesque but somehow apposite sense that overpowering horror has intensified reality into theatre, contains an insight into the performative element that inhabits all social existence. Dickens's characterisation has been criticised as failing to match the psychological realism achieved by George Eliot in her representation of a complex inner life. But Dickens's concern is with the equally complex, performative patterns of external behaviour by means of which non-rational states of mind and hidden identities are articulated.

A more extended characterisation that draws upon the same sources of fairy tale and popular culture and the same psychological insights is that of the witch-like figure of Miss Havisham in *Great Expectations* (1861). Miss Havisham has turned her life into a spectacular theatre of decay, even choreographing the climactic scene after her death when her body will be laid upon the table set for the bridal meal and her greedy relatives summoned to feast upon her (Dickens 1965: ch. 11, 116). Fantastic though the figure is, it does not relinquish realism's concern with the individual character as a location of social forces. The disturbing image of age-wasted bride offers a powerful symbolic rendering of the self-denying, withered existence imposed upon many middle-class women in Victorian England. Dickens's imaginative representation has its non-fictional counterpart in Florence Nightingale's embittered secret writing in her unpublished essay *Cassandra* (1852). (Strachey [1928] 1978 contains the text of *Cassandra*, which was not published during Nightingale's own life.) *Great Expectations* was published in 1861, the same year as the death of Prince Albert. Following his death, Queen Victoria transformed her life into a royal performance of grief that kept her secluded from any public appearance for years.

BRITISH DEBATES ON REALISM

By the mid-1860s almost all of the major realist writing of the nineteenth century had been achieved. Dickens's last complete novel, *Our Mutual Friend*, was published in 1865 and Gaskell died that year with *Wives and Daughters* not quite concluded. Thackeray had died in 1863 and Charlotte Brontë in 1855, well outliving her sisters. Eliot published *Middlemarch* in 1871–2 and *Daniel Deronda* in 1874–6 but only Thomas Hardy still had his career to make in the last part of the century. So it is somewhat paradoxical that the main artistic debates about realism only reached Britain from France in the 1880s. From the more aware artistic consciousness of that era, it seemed to writers like Henry James (1843–1916), George Gissing (1857–1903) and Robert Louis Stevenson (1850–94) that the earlier novelists had practised the craft of novel-writing blithely unaware of aesthetic considerations. According to Henry James, 'there was a comfortable, good-humoured feeling abroad that a novel is a novel, as a pudding is a pudding, and that our only business with it could be to swallow it' (James [1894] 1987: 187). James rather overstates the case here. Throughout the nineteenth century, the periodical press carried long, serious review articles on novels. (Graham 1965 and Stang 1959 provide details of critical debates on novels during the second half of the nineteenth century.) However, it is true that realism as such was not a central issue of aesthetic concern. Yet the first use of the term in Britain, when *Frazer's Magazine* described Thackeray as 'chief of the Realist School', just predates the passionate French controversy over the term '*réalisme*' sparked off by Gustave Courbet in 1855. In 1853, *The Westminster Review* printed a long admiring essay on 'Balzac and his Writing', recognising him as 'head of the realist school in France' (Evans 1853: 203). In recommending his work as such to British readers, the reviewer gives absolutely no indication that there might be anything controversial about such a mode of writing. Indeed, the reviewer comments that in England, spared 'the infliction of an Academy', the 'literary warfare' that met Balzac's work could 'scarcely be comprehended' (Evans 1853: 202–3).

Certainly on the whole, debates around realism in Britain during the 1880s and 1890s were typified by pragmatic moderation rather than artistic, let alone political, passion. Three main issues were involved: the comparative merits of realism to those of romance and idealism, a demand for more concern with formal aspects of fictional art, and what was seen as the affront to moral decency in naturalistic novels. In an essay entitled 'Realism in Art: Recent German Fiction', published in *The Westminster Review* in 1858, G. H. Lewes, the life-partner of George Eliot, argued that all 'Art is a Representation of Reality' and so it follows that 'Realism is thus the basis of all Art, and its antithesis is not Idealism, but *Falsism*' (Lewes 1858: 494). Lewes's thinking shows quite clearly the influence of romanticism on British notions of 'truth' and 'reality'. Great painters and writers, Lewes argues, convey images of real things and people but these are intensified by the artist's poetic sensibility. By this means, without departing from strict accuracy of external detail, they produce art which is 'in the highest sense ideal, and which is so because it is also in the highest sense real' (Lewes 1858: 494). In the 1880s, there was a resurgence of interest in the romance genre, stories of high adventure, often set in exotic locations of the Empire, inhabited by strange peoples. Robert Louis Stevenson (1850–94) was regarded as one of the chief exponents of romance but in his critical writing, he, too, refused to see realism in an oppositional light. In 'A Note on Realism' (1885), he sets out a view very close to that of G.H. Lewes: 'All representative art, which can be said to live, is both realistic and ideal' (Stevenson 1999: 67). George Gissing (1857–1903) was influenced by the French naturalism of Zola, yet he reiterated the same point in his book on Dickens, 'But there can be drawn only a misleading, futile distinction between novels realistic and idealistic. It is merely a question of degree and of the author's temperament' (Gissing 1898: 218). Henry James magisterially dismissed the 'celebrated distinction between the novel and the romance...There are bad novels and good novels, as there are bad pictures and good pictures; but that is the only distinction in which I can see any meaning' (James [1894] 1987: 196).

James was passionately concerned with what makes a good novel and, although he says in 'The Art of Fiction' that 'the air of reality (solidity of specification) seems to me to be the supreme virtue of a novel', it is obvious from the prefaces he wrote to his own fiction and from his essays on other novelists, that he set a very high premium on the kind of self-conscious craftsmanship practised by a writer like Flaubert (James [1894] 1987: 195). R. L. Stevenson was also influenced by French artistic concern and he, too, favoured greater attention to artistic form, insisting, in his essay 'A Humble Remonstrance', that while 'Life is monstrous, infinite, illogical, abrupt, and poignant; a work of art in comparison, is neat, finite, self-contained, rational, flowing and emasculate' (Stevenson 1999: 85). Given the terms in which

Stevenson sets up this opposition between art and life, most of his readers might well opt for life. Art for art's sake was never articulated with such conviction as in France. The move towards greater formalism by British modernists at the beginning of the twentieth century was probably influenced more by the work of French novelists and poets and by the fictional practices of James and Conrad than by public critical debates.

Public passion over the issue of realism was only aroused by what was seen as an attack upon the foundations of British morality. For much of the nineteenth century Mudie's Circulating Library (1842–1937), which claimed to purchase 180,000 volumes a year, had effectively operated a system of censorship by refusing to stock any literature likely to cause offence as family reading. Since library sales constituted a very substantial part of any author's earnings, all writers were forced to conform to Mudie's conventional moral code. However, by the 1880s, cheap mass publication had put an end to Mudie's control of the book market and the publisher Vizetelly hoped to cash in on Zola's fame or notoriety by publishing English translations of his work. In response, the National Vigilance Association launched a vociferous campaign to suppress such 'pernicious literature'. Attacks on the 'filth' and 'obscenity' which were projected as a threat to national life appeared in the religious, local and national press. There was a debate on the matter in Parliament in May, 1888 and a criminal case was taken out against Vizetelly who voluntarily undertook to withdraw all offending literature from sale. (Becker 1963 reprints the transcript of the debate in Parliament as it was published by the National Vigilance Association; Becker: 350–382 also provides extracts from newspaper items of the affair. Keating 1989: 241–84 contains a good account of the Vizetelly prosecution and of end-of-century challenges to forms of moral censorship.) This incident was but the most extreme example of the moral conformity that had governed British public life during the whole century and beyond. Balzac had much earlier noted that Walter Scott was false in his portrayal of women because he was 'obliged to conform to the ideas of an essentially hypocritical country' (Balzac 1981: 142). In his Preface to *Pendennis* (1850), Thackeray complained that 'Since the author of *Tom Jones* was buried, no writer of fiction among us has been permitted to depict to his utmost power a

MAN....Society will not tolerate the natural in art.' (Thackeray [1850] 1994: lvi). Gissing makes the same point in comparing Dickens's work to that of Dostoevsky, and James acknowledges the selective principle of Mrs Grundy as symbol of Victorian proprieties (Gissing 1898: 223; James [1894] 1987: 200).

THOMAS HARDY AND THE CULMINATION OF BRITISH NINETEENTH-CENTURY REALISM

Thomas Hardy (1840–1928) was heir to the achievements of the earlier generations of nineteenth-century realists and to the later debates deriving from French realism. Hardy wrote in defiance of Victorian proprieties, attempting to incorporate into his fiction the aspects of human experience, most notably those concerned with sexuality, that his predecessors had been forced to avoid. As a result, his novels, especially *Tess of the D'Urbervilles* (1891) and *Jude the Obscure* (1895) were met with outrage and denunciations. Yet in the commercial literary market-place that had come into existence by the end of the century, Hardy, like Zola, discovered that notoriety meant sales. (Keating 1989: 369–445 describes the rise of the 'best seller'.) He made enough money from *Jude the Obscure* to give up novel writing and turn to the poorer financial rewards but greater cultural capital of poetry. Hardy also resembled Zola in accepting a Darwinian perception of a social and physical universe ruled by the harsh laws of natural selection and heredity. Again like his fellow French writer, critics have judged those parts of his work that most clearly conform to such a 'scientific' perspective the least artistically successful. As critic Gillian Beer (1983) has shown, the more creative and pervasive influence of Darwin's *On the Origin of Species* (1859) on British novelists was an imaginative grasp of evolutionary forms of change, historical and natural, and an absorption of Darwin's own metaphors for natural forces. The great insight that Hardy's realism gained from Darwin resides in a very complex sense of time. The poeticising of his historical imagination enables him to embody intensely particularised individual characters within a vast sweep of change from primeval to present time as inscribed on the panoramic surface of landscape. It is this symbolic intensification of the localised individual as historical type caught up in an unending process of change that is one of Hardy's unique contributions to realism not his occasional depiction of character as mechanically determined by physical and social laws.

Raymond Williams argues that Hardy uses his major characters to explore new novelistic territory: his protagonists inhabit the insecure border country between familiar, customary patterns of life and the unmapped mobility of new social formations (Williams 1974: 81). 'Territory' is a precise term since the characters' insecurities are always materialised as geographical dislocation and unsettlement. In *Tess of the D'Urbervilles*, Tess and Angel Clare travel by horse and cart through the remote and ancient landscape of Egdon Heath to deliver milk to the new railway station:

> They crept along towards a point in the expanse of shade just at hand at which a feeble light was beginning to assert its presence; a spot where, by day, a fitful white streak of steam at intervals upon the dark green background denoted intermittent moments of contact between their secluded world and modern life. Modern life stretched out its steam feeler to this point three or four times a day, touched the native existences and quickly withdrew its feeler again, as if what it touched had been uncongenial.
>
> They reached the feeble light which came from the smokey lamp of a little railway station; a poor enough terrestrial star, yet in one sense of more importance to Talbothays Dairy and mankind than the celestial ones to which it stood in such humiliating contrast. The cans of new milk were unladen in the rain, Tess getting a little shelter from a neighbouring holly-tree.
>
> Then there was a hissing of a train which drew up almost silently upon the wet rails, and the milk was rapidly swung can by can into the truck. The light of the engine flashed for a second upon Tess Durbeyfield's figure, motionless under the great holly-tree. [...] Tess was so receptive that the few minutes of contact with the whirl of material progress lingered in her thought.
>
> 'Londoners will drink it at their breakfast tomorrow, won't they?' she asked. 'Strange people that we have never seen.'
>
> (Hardy [1891] 1988: 187–8)

Typically, Hardy's language renders an intellectual insight into the incompatibility of traditional and modern worlds as palpable experience: the creeping pace of the cart juxtaposed to the 'fitful'...'steam feeler' quickly pulling back from contact with what is felt as uncongenially other. Yet the apparently idyllic world of Talbothays Dairy (which can so easily be idealised as 'timelessly' rural) depends, for the viability of its large-scale milk production, upon the new transportation system that brings London consumers within a few hours reach. In this passage, as elsewhere in the novel, Tess is at the juncture of these two historical worlds and, as her question indicates, is perceived as a consciousness percipient of both. The historicised understanding of character is made yet more complex by the association of Tess in Hardy's writing with a rich tradition of fairy tale and popular culture, as here in the representation of her figure picked out in light 'motionless under the great holly-tree'. Without sacrificing any of the precise location of Tess at the point of junction between a newly forming mass consumer mobility and a more slow-paced agricultural society, this understructure of myth and folk tradition reminds us of the unending process of historical change and all those numberless and nameless individuals who have found themselves haplessly on insecure border territory.

A final point to notice about the passage is that Hardy makes no attempt to offer a rational account or objective analysis of just how Tess's consciousness is shaped by her perception of two worlds. Realism neither requires nor claims certainty. In practice, it does not aim at scientific or objective truth, and most especially its goal is not any authoritative or singular notion of truth. Its use of surface detail is governed by poetic selection and historicising imagination not documentary inventory. Its predominant mode is comic, irreverent, secular and sceptical. Realism is capacious enough to recognise that social realities are multiple and constructed; it is formally adventurous enough to incorporate non-realist genres like fairy tale, romanticism and melodrama, appropriating their qualities to realist ends. However, the project of realism is founded upon an implicit consensual belief that realities do exist 'out there' beyond linguistic networks and that we can use language to explore and communicate our always incomplete knowledge of that ever-changing historical materiality. Thus, the form of realism is necessarily protean but the commitment of the genre to historical particularity is non-negotiable.

III

LITERARY REALISM AS FORMAL ART

5

REALITY EFFECTS

We saw in Part I that during the twentieth century the tradition of realist writing came under criticism from first a modernist and then a postmodernist perspective. At the centre of these critiques is an accusation that literary realism practises a form of dishonesty, veiling its status as art to suggest it is simply a copy or reflection of life. In so doing, its critics claim, it shores up the complacency of assumed notions and prejudices about the world rather than producing challenging new forms of knowledge. In Part II, I aimed to show that the development of the realist novel during the nineteenth-century was characterised by continuous experimentation with narrative techniques, by democratisation of subject matter and often by confrontation with authority. Yet the very success of realism as a form means that we do now rather tend to take it for granted. One of the main aims of Part III, therefore, is to look more closely at the intrinsic, formal aspects of realist writing in order to appreciate more fully the artistic achievement of creating the effect of 'being just like life'.

Formalism is an approach to art that focuses primarily upon immanent or inherent, self-contained aspects of the artistic form and structure of a work rather than its extrinsic relationship to actuality. In the early part of the twentieth century, formalism was developed as the preferred approach to literature in both America and Russia. Although American New Critics and Russian Formalists pursued quite different agendas and were unaware of each other's existence, they shared a common belief that the study of literature needed to aspire to the objective status of science. (For a succinct account of New Criticism see Robey 1986 or Selden 1985.) By the beginning of the twentieth century, the growing prestige of scientific disciplines as a means of furthering human knowledge, made former approaches to literary study seem amateurish and lacking requisite objectivity. In order to emulate the success of science, it was argued, literary studies must be defined by a rigorous focus upon the literary text itself as its sole object of investigation. In elaborating their quite different critical methodologies for approaching this scientific ideal, American New Critics tended to concern themselves predominantly with poetry while Russian Formalism encompassed a wider perspective of the literary. Moreover, Russian Formalism had a formative influence on the subsequent development of structuralism. In this chapter, therefore, I shall map this critical history from Russian Formalism to French poststructuralism, focusing upon those aspects of formal analysis that are most immediately applicable to literary realism.

In adopting a scientific model, both Russian Formalists and later structuralists rejected any concern with the value of literature or of the values inscribed in literary texts. In pursuing knowledge of molecular structures, for example, scientists do not ask whether these are good or bad, progressive or repressive, their concern is with how the molecular system functions. By analogy, for Russian Formalists and for structuralists the key question for literary studies is not what does a text mean? or how fine is the writing? but how does it work? how does it produce meaning? Yet, when the linguistic 'turn' of structuralism was displaced by the cultural 'turn' of poststructuralism, this scientific approach was seen as mistaken. The formal aspects of a work, no less than its content, were understood to carry 'meaning' in the sense of sustaining those underlying structures that produce the unquestioned ideological assumptions mapping our reality. To take a simple example, we have noted how the 'closed' structure of many realist novels, the culmination of the plot in resolution of all mysteries and uncertainties, functions to reassure us that human existence is ultimately meaningful. The formal analyses of poststructural critics, therefore, aim to reveal the means by which realist texts produce the illusion of reality that functions to confirm our expectations. Yet, I shall argue, if the formal aspects and structures of texts frequently work to produce a comforting sense of the world as we expect it to be, it follows that they can, by these same formal structures, draw attention to underlying epistemological assumptions that shape our perception of social reality, de-naturalising these structures so that they become visible to us and we are able to think beyond their limits. The second aim of this chapter, then, is to investigate both the artistic means by which literary realism achieves the effects of an already existing actuality and the extent to which it discomforts presuppositions, encouraging us to challenge or rethink them.

For Russian Formalists the first issue of importance was to define the object of their study: what constituted the literariness of literary texts? Or, what makes literary language different in kind from everyday use of language? This led Victor Shklovsky, in an influential essay, 'Art as Technique' (1917), to distinguish poetic or literary language as that which makes use of techniques of estrangement or defamiliarisation (reprinted in Lodge 1988: 20, 21). Whereas everyday language and experience rests upon processes of habituation so that perception becomes automatic, literary language shocks us into seeing the familiar with fresh eyes. For Shklovsky, the triumph of Tolstoy's realism is that he brings a shocking strangeness to his representation of the world: 'He describes an object as if he were seeing it for the first time' (Lodge 1988: 21).

Ferdinand de Saussure's structural linguistics was known to Russian Formalists and shaped the work of two critics who were influential within the later structuralist movement in France: Vladimir Propp (1895–1970) and Roman Jakobson (1896–1982). Just as Saussure had suggested that the vast multiplicity of 'parole', that is actual speech utterances, were produced by an underlying grammar or 'langue', so structural narratologists, like Propp, hoped to discover the limited set of rules that produce the numerous diversity of stories that human beings have created throughout history. In his early structuralist essay, 'Introduction to Structuralist Analysis of Narratives' (1966) Roland Barthes points out: 'The narratives of the world are numberless...under [an]...almost infinite diversity of forms, narrative is present in every age, in every place, in every society; it begins with the very history of mankind and there nowhere is or has been a people without narrative' (Barthes 1977: 79). Barthes goes on to point admiringly to Propp's analysis of over a hundred Russian folk tales to isolate just thirty-two recurrent constitutive narrative elements that he calls 'functions' (Propp [1929] 1971: 91–114; Propp 1968: 21). So, for example, in fairy tales the element of 'the gift' performs the constant function of enabling the hero to accomplish his 'task' which is another constitutive function. The exact nature of the gift or task and who gives or performs it is immaterial to the structural function of each element which remains identical in all the tales. The project to establish **narratology** as a science was strongest during the 1960s and into the 1970s, substantiated in the work of Seymour Chapman (1978) and A.J. Greimas (1971) as well as Propp. (An account of their work can be found in Culler 1975, Rimmon-Kenan 1983. Currie 1998 gives a highly readable account of more recent theoretical approaches to narrative.) Thereafter, enthusiasm for the enterprise faltered somewhat: no generally accepted 'grammar' able to account for all forms of narrative could be found and more importantly that goal came to seem reductive and mistaken. It aimed to translate the rich multiplicity of the world's stories into rather banal elements like 'functions' and it was indifferent to the cultural specificity of texts and to the ideological functioning of narrative structure.

Roman Jakobson was probably the most important figure bridging the theoretical endeavours of Russian Formalism and French structuralism. His work is primarily linguistic not literary, but he was centrally concerned, like other Russian Formalists, to define the distinctive nature of poetic language. 'On Realism in Art' (1921) is the only essay in which he specifically addressed the topic of realism. His main concern was to point out how, of all literary forms, realism is the least likely to be objectively defined and evaluated. 'We call realistic', he says, 'those works which we feel accurately depict life by displaying verisimilitude' (Jakobson [1921] 1971: 38). Yet more often than not this so-called aesthetic judgement simply means that the reader agrees with the view of reality that the text offers. Jakobson is arguing for the need of an objective definition of realism. He does not come up with one, but his recognition of the ideological investments embedded in praises of a work's realism looks prophetically forward to the rigid artistic doctrine of **socialist realism** adopted by the Congress of Soviet Writers in 1934 at the behest of Stalin. Socialist realism conveyed as reality only heroic proletarian protagonists in plots of always ultimately optimistic struggle;

any form of experimentalism was denounced as decadent. It was Georg Lukács's attempt to justify this Soviet attack upon modernist art that led to the public quarrel with the critics of the Frankfurt School outlined in Chapter 1.

Jakobson's most influential contribution to structuralist poetics was contained in his important essay on 'Linguistics and Poetics' (1960). In this work he provides a valuable insight into one way in which literary texts convey a 'reality effect'. Before turning to this essay, I shall contextualise my use of the term 'effect'. By the 1970s Roland Barthes had rejected the structuralist enterprise. In *S/Z* (1973), which comprises a detailed textual dissection of Balzac's story, *Sarrasine*, he declares that the goal of discovering a common grammar underlying all narratives is 'a task as exhausting...as it is ultimately undesirable, for the text thereby loses its difference' (Barthes [1973] 1990: 3). What Barthes is implicitly acknowledging is the particularity of detail that constitutes the distinctive quality of realist writing, its fascination with the diverse multiplicity of the material world. In *S/Z* he claims that the very gratuitousness of apparently insignificant detail in a realist story 'serves to authenticate the fiction by means of what we call the *reality effect* (Barthes [1973] 1990: 182. He discusses this device at greater length in 'The Reality Effect', Barthes 1960: 11–17.) Borrowing Barthes' term, I shall outline, in the rest of this chapter, the artistic means by which literary realism authenticates itself in terms that I call the empirical effect, the truth effect and the character effect.

THE EMPIRICAL EFFECT

By the empirical effect I mean all those techniques by which realist writing seems to convey the experiential actuality of existence in physical space and chronological time. In novels this spatial and temporal reality has to be transposed or translated into the order of words as they traverse the space of the page and as the linear sequence in which they are read. In 'Linguistics and Poetics' (1960), Roman Jakobson argues that all language is governed by two fundamental principles: that of combination and that of selection (Jakobson 1960: 358). The rules of syntax govern the way in which words can be combined together to form a grammatical sentence: the combination of 'The elephant packed her trunk' forms a meaningful sequence, whereas 'Packed her the elephant trunk' does not. In addition to the principle of orderly combination, the sentence is also formed by means of selecting an appropriate word at each point of the syntactic sequence. Instead of 'elephant' as the subject of the sentence, 'rhino' could be selected or 'holiday maker' or any other word able to function in a similar or paradigmatic way. Equally the verb 'packed' could be replaced by 'filled' or 'locked' or some other selected word able to fill that place in the combinational or syntagmatic sequence. Whereas the principle of selection is governed by recognition of similarity, the principle of combination is governed by rules of contiguity, of what can come next to what. Jakobson calls the selection of words from similar sets of words the paradigmatic axis of language and the combination of words into a contiguous order of syntax, the syntagmatic axis. To make the complicated more complex still, he associates the combinational or syntagmatic axis with the figure of speech known as metonymy and the selective or paradigmatic axis with metaphor. This is because metaphor is also based upon a principle of selecting for similarity: 'His words were pure gold' metaphorically associates the metal 'gold' with the apparently disparate term 'words' because of the perceived similarity of high value.

Metonymy, on the other hand, is based upon the perception of contiguity. In metonymy an attribute of something comes to stand for the whole. One of the most familiar figures of metonymy is when the term 'crown' is used as a way of referring to the monarch as in rhetorical declarations of the 'dignity of the crown' or 'the crown in parliament'. Subsumed within Jakobson's use of the term metonymy is the figure of speech known as synecdoche which is based even more closely upon contiguity since it substitutes a part of the whole for the entirety: in a phrase like 'all hands on deck', the term 'hands' stand for the whole bodies and persons being called upon to help. 'The crowned heads of Europe' might accordingly be seen as drawing upon the figures of both synecdoche and metonymy.

What has all this to do with realism? Well, Jakobson defined poetic functioning of language as that in which the paradigmatic or metaphorical axis of selection based upon similarity comes to dominate the combinational or syntagmatic axis based upon contiguity. The poetic function, Jakobson stressed, is not confined to what would normally be recognised as poetry or even as canonical literature more generally. The poetic function exists whereever the axis of selection takes predominance over that of contiguity; Jakobson quotes the political slogan 'I like Ike' as an example of the poetic function in non-literary discourse (Jakobson 1960: 357). Most of Jakobson's exposition of the poetic function in 'Linguistics and Poetics' is taken up with illustrations of the ways the principle of selection is governed by recognition of similarity: metaphorical comparisons, rhyme, rhythm, phrasing and sound repetitions, ambiguous playing upon double meanings. Almost as an aside, he remarks that while there has been considerable study of poetic metaphor, 'so-called realistic literature, intimately tied with the metonymic principle, still defies interpretation' (Jakobson 1960: 375). In another essay on 'Two Aspects of Language and Two Types of Aphasic Disturbances' (1956) he returns to the idea, arguing that 'it is still insufficiently realised that it is the predominance of metonymy which underlies and actually determines the so-called "realist" trend.' (reprinted in Lodge 1988: 31–61)

Unfortunately, Jakobson did not develop these suggestions further but perhaps an example will clarify the connection of metonymy, as a principle of contiguity, with the empirical effect of realist writing. Here is a passage from a modern novel, *Grace Notes* (1998) by Bernard MacLaverty, in which the young female protagonist flies home to Ireland on the death of her father.

When they dropped down through the cloud at Aldergrove she saw how green the land was. And how small the fields. A mosaic of vivid greens and yellows and browns. Home. She wanted to cry again.

The bus into Belfast was stopped at a checkpoint and a policeman in a flak jacket, a young guy with a ginger moustache, walked up the aisle towards her, his head moving in a slow no as he looked from side to side, from seat to opposite seat for bombs. He winked at her, 'Cheer up love, it might never happen.'

But it already had.

On the bus home she watched the familiar landmarks she used as a child pass one by one. Toomebridge, her convent school, the drop into low gear to take the hill out of Magherafelt.

> The bus stopped at a crossroads on the outskirts of her home town and a woman got off. Before she walked away, the driver and she had a conversation, shouted over the engine noise. This was the crossroads where the Orangemen held their drumming matches. It was part of her childhood to look up from the kitchen table on still Saturday evenings and hear the rumble of the drums. Her mother would roll her eyes, 'They're at it again'.
>
> (MacLaverty 1998: 6–7)

Jakobson noted that as well as realist writing, film is also a medium in which the metonymic principle predominates (Lodge 1988: 59). It is easy to recognise how cinematic the above passage is. The sentences could be translated directly into a visual medium that would show an almost seamless contiguous tracking movement through space: the plane dropping down through the air, the land moving in closer, the passenger transferring to bus, the policeman walking slowly from the front of the bus to the back, the bus drive through landscape, passing one feature after another. This movement through contiguous space can be mapped almost automatically by the reader on to a contiguous passage through chronological time from the moment of the descent of the plane to the time of arrival home. The empirical effect achieved by *Grace Notes* in this extract derives very largely from the dominance of the metonymic principle which organises the writing. The critic David Lodge, who has developed Jakobson's analysis of literary language in terms of opposing metaphoric and metonymic modes of writing, has pointed out that all literary texts are ultimately absorbed by metaphor when we come to speak of the general values that the work as a whole seems to express (Lodge 1977: 109–11). In the case of the passage from *Grace Notes* we might want to understand it as representing 'grief' or 'exile' and in that sense it would be functioning metaphorically not metonymically. Nevertheless, what is specific and valuable about realist writing is the way the principle of contiguity pushes any over-facile universalising tendency of metaphor into a very tense balance with historical particularity. The particularised, empirical effect of *Grace Notes*, its here and now feel, resists any complacent or comforting translation of its meaning into the commonplaces of a timeless human nature.

In *S/Z*, Roland Barthes performs an almost microscopic structural study of Balzac's story, *Sarrasine*, by analysing very small semantic units (lexias) in terms of five codes or voices that interweave to constitute the text (Barthes [1973] 1990: 13). Two of these codes participate closely in the empirical effect: the first he calls the code of actions or the voice of empirics, and the second is the cultural or referential code or the voice of science. The code of actions can be associated with the principle of contiguity since the code provides names or titles that embody an empirical sequence of events such as 'answering a knock at the door'. Barthes says that 'to read is to struggle to name' and the code of actions allows readers to recognise and name contiguous empirical sequences and this 'recognition' has the effect of authenticating the experiential validity of the text. In the extract from *Grace Notes* readers will automatically recognise and name the narrative sequences as 'taking a flight', 'returning home' or 'going to a funeral' and in addition to allowing readers to recognise with a name and thus seem to authenticate the sequence from their own experience, it also fulfils their expectations of the order of events in the sequence and the need for an end to each sequential chain. It thus implies that the sequence unfolds within the temporal contiguity of linear time. This concordance of events into meaningful recognisable sequences can be thought of as constituting a structure of intelligibility. Barthes calls this fulfilment of the principle of contiguity an operation of solidarity whereby everything seems to hold together: the text is 'controlled by the principle of non-contradiction,...by stressing at every opportunity the *compatible* nature of circumstance, by attaching narrated events together with a kind of logical "paste"' (Barthes [1973] 1990: 156). We can perceive the extract from *Grace Notes* as 'pasted' into an intelligible solidarity by means of its logical and empirical contiguities.

The second code that contributes to the empirical effect of realist writing is what Barthes calls the cultural or referential code and, less appositely, the voice of science. By cultural code, he understands all those multiple explicit and implicit references in a text: familiar cultural knowledge, proverbial wisdom, commonsensical assumptions, school texts, stereotypical thinking. By means of a dense network of citation to such cultural sources of information a text 'form[s] an oddly joined miniature version of encyclopaedic knowledge, a farrago...[of] everyday "reality"' (Barthes [1973] 1990: 185). In *Grace Notes* this 'farrago' is made up of references to Irish place names, military knowledge as to what is a 'flak jacket', historical recognition of the significance of 'Orangemen' and drumming, awareness of the need to change a vehicle's gears on hills and the familiar gestural language in which rolling eyes signifies shared irony. This web of citation evokes what Barthes calls a sense of repleteness; the text seems to share the semantic fullness of a known social reality.

Although Barthes recognises a code of actions that names a sequence of events, he pays little attention to the complex handling of time in narrative which is one of the great achievements of realist writing, techniques subsequently developed and extended by modernist novelists. Gerard Genette provides the most systematic structural analysis of narrative time in *Narrative Discourse: An Essay in Method* (1980) which is a detailed study of Marcel Proust's novel *Remembrance of Things Past* (1913–27). Genette begins by making a clear distinction between story time and narrative time: in this context 'story time' refers to the abstracted chronological chain of events upon which the actual spoken or written narrative is based, whereas 'narrative time' refers to the handling of that story chronology in the specific telling of the tale (Genette 1980: 35). Consider for example, the sequential chain of events that constitutes the traditional story 'Cinderella': her mother dies, her father remarries, her step-mother and step-sisters ill-treat her, they go to the ball without her, she is visited by her fairy god-mother, she goes to the ball and meets the prince. In an actual narrative, this abstract or 'natural' chronological sequence of the story can be re-ordered many ways. The narrative could begin with marriage to the prince and then look back on the events leading up to the happy ending or it could begin with Cinderella left alone while the family goes to the ball, look back to the beginning and then proceed to the ending of the story. In addition, a narrative can linger far longer over one event than another; the scene of the ball might take up more than half the narrative with the other events recounted briefly. Genette reminds us that this complex arrangement of temporal relationships in narrative exists primarily in space: the material space of the lines of the text on the page and the only real time involved is 'the time needed for *crossing* or *traversing* it, like a road or a field. The narrative text, like every other text, has no temporality than what it borrows, metonymically, from its own reading' (Genette 1980: 34). Genette's account of narrative time is extremely detailed and substantiated by close reading of Proust's text. Here, I shall only outline those points that contribute most directly to the empirical effect.

The main disruptions that narrative order makes to story order is that of flashbacks to earlier events or foreshadowings of what is to yet come. Genette terms narrative flashback 'analepsis' and anticipatory segments 'prolepsis' (Genette 1980: 40). In addition, narrative can make use of external analepsis and prolepsis which are so-called because they reach beyond the beginning and ending of the temporal span of the main narrative. Novelistic prose typically organises these temporal relationships in very complex ways. Although time is often thought of as a one-way linear flow from past towards the future, our actual empirical experience of temporality is much more complicated than this. Frequently our current actions are determined by participation of their future effect and by memory of previous events. Similarly a present event may give a completely new meaning to something that occurred in the past.

The ordering of time in realist narratives authenticates an empirical effect by simultaneously meeting readers' expectations of the orderly sequence required for intelligibility and their sense of temporal anachrony, the disorder of strict linear progression. In her novel, *The Prime of Miss Jean Brodie*, (1961), Muriel Spark (1918–) utilises an extremely skilful and subtle play with the order of narrative time. In this extract, from early in the novel, Miss Brodie is holding her class in the garden of Marcia Blaine School:

> She leant against the elm. It was one of the last autumn days when the leaves were falling in little gusts. They fell on the children who were thankful for this excuse to wriggle and for the allowable movements in brushing the leaves from their hair and laps.
>
> 'Season of mists and mellow fruitfulness. I was engaged to a young man at the beginning of the War but he fell on Flanders' Field', said Miss Brodie. 'Are you thinking, Sandy, of doing a day's washing?'
>
> 'No, Miss Brodie.'
>
> 'Because you have got your sleeves rolled up. I won't have to do with girls who roll up the sleeves of their blouses, however fine the

weather. Roll them down at once, we are civilized beings. He fell the week before Armistice was declared. He fell like an autumn leaf, although he was only twenty-two years of age. When we go indoors we shall look on the map at Flanders, and the spot where my lover was laid before you were born. [...]

The story of Miss Brodie's felled fiance was well on its way when the headmistress, Miss Mackay, was seen to approach across the lawn. Tears had already started to drop from Sandy's little pig-like eyes and Sandy's tears now affected her friend Jenny, later famous in the school for her beauty, who gave a sob and groped up the leg of her knickers for her handkerchief. 'Hugh was killed', said Miss Brodie, 'a week before Armistice. After that there was a general election and people were saying 'Hang the Kaiser!' Hugh was one of the Flowers of the Forest, lying in his grave.' Rose Stanley had now begun to weep. Sandy slid her wet eyes sideways, watching the advance of Miss Mackay, head and shoulders forward, across the lawn.

(Spark 1965: 12–13)

As our eyes traverse the linear progress of the passage on the page we can map this semantically onto an intelligible sequence of events in linear narrative time. According to Barthes' code of actions we recognise the sequence as the somewhat subversive activity of 'taking a school lesson outside', followed by an expected sequence 'interruption by authority'. This logical and temporal contiguity performs what Barthes calls an operation of solidarity that provides the passage with a firm ligature of intelligibility. Yet within this framework, temporal order becomes very complex indeed. Miss Brodie's reference to the death of her fiancee at Flanders is an external analepsis, looking back to a time before the beginning of the actual narrative. Her quotation from Keat's 'Ode to Autumn' could perhaps been seen as an even longer reach of analepsis beyond the scope of story time altogether. In contrast, her plan to find the spot on the schoolroom map that marks where her lover fell is an internal prolepsis looking forward to an imminent event when the class returns indoors. The reference to Jenny's later fame in the school for her beauty is also an internal prolepsis but one that reaches further into the future of narrative time. This interweaving of past, present and future narrative time is made yet more complex by the insertion of deictic words like 'now' into the narrative past tense. Deictics are words that seem to point to or be referring to an immediately present spatial or temporal context. Thus although the sentences 'Sandy's tears now affected her friend Jenny' and 'Rose Stanley had now begun to weep' are related in the past tense, the deictic 'now' conveys a sense of unfolding presentness.

In addition to sequence of events, realist narratives also carefully manipulate the representation of temporal duration and frequency to authenticate the empirical effect. In lived experience time does not appear to pass at the same regular pace: some events seem to stretch out for hours while others flit by almost unnoticed. The allocation of narrative space is used to convey this subjective experience of time passing; yet by the same means realist writing can foreground this relativism of time and throw it into question. Realist texts frequently use narrative repetition to challenge simplistic views of reality: an event retold from different perspectives suggests that truth may be shifting and even multiple. A more complex and interesting organisation of relations of frequency utilised by realist writers is the fusion of reiteration with a singular event. This occurs in *Grace Notes* when the narrative refers to an oft repeated pattern that 'was part of her childhood to look up from the kitchen table on still Saturday evenings and hear the rumble of the drums.' This produces the effect of a customary texture of life in which events become habitual through repetition. But the next sentence moves into the particularity of her mother's speech, 'They're at it again.' Presumably she did not parrot this on each and every occasion. The effect produced is a simultaneous sense of quite particular empirical specificity and an encompassing social world. This duality of focus from particular to general, I shall argue, is a defining and inherently challenging characteristic of realist writing.

THE TRUTH EFFECT

Despite this here and now feel of realist novels, they do seem frequently to be offering us more than just forms of empirical knowledge of particularised lives within a more generalised social milieu. They seem often to imply truth claims of a more universal philosophical or ethical nature. This is what I term the truth effect and it functions ideologically to affirm the availability, ultimately, of at least a degree of knowledge and enlightenment within the order of human existence. Many critics have come to see the human desire to impose meaning on the chaos of existence as the impulse underlying the ubiquity of narrative in all times and places. It is the strong desire for order which keeps us turning the pages, hurrying onwards to the resolution of all mystery and confusions promised at the conclusion of the tale. For this reason the detective story is often seen as the narrative of narratives in that it is the genre which reveals most explicitly the quest for truth impelling all fictions. Barthes understands two of his five codes as particularly involved in this truth effect: the hermeneutic code that he otherwise calls the voice of truth and the symbolic code or field.

Novels typically begin by raising some question in the reader's mind that immediately compels them to follow the plot (the word is suggestive) for clues that will unravel the mystery or clarify the puzzle. Clearly such enigmas cannot be solved too quickly or the story would be over. So although a realist narrative must appear to be structured upon the forward progression of historical time, the hermeneutic code must continually frustrate these expectations and invent delaying tactics, lay false clues and set snares for the reader. It is only at the conclusion of the reading that the reader can look back and make sense of the whole pattern of events. Thus, although the narrative appears to construct a forward linear movement, it simultaneously inscribes a reverse projection backwards. The effect of teasing the reader with delayed enlightenment is to strengthen the belief that 'truth' does exist and will prevail however difficult the passage towards it proves to be. As Barthes comments, 'Expectation thus becomes the basic condition for truth: truth, these narratives tell us, is what is *at the end* of expectation' ([1973] 1990: 76). In other words, we could say that desire for truth produces our belief in truth.

Barthes claims that the hermeneutic code works in tandem with the symbolic field of the text to convey a sense of truth that moves beyond the horizons of the particular. This is best explained by means of an illustration. The title of Charles Dickens's novel, *Great Expectations*, (1861) immediately suggests its involvement in the process of anticipation and the opening pages of the story provide one of the most startling eruptions of an enigma in fiction. The adult narrator, begins his story, with the early moment in his childhood when he first becomes aware of his own identity and his orphaned state.

> My first most vivid and broad impression of the identity of things, seems to me to have been gained on a memorable raw afternoon towards evening. At such a time I found out for certain, that this bleak place overgrown with nettles was the churchyard; and that Philip Pirrip, late of this parish, and also Georgiana wife of the above, were dead and buried;...and that the flat dark wilderness beyond the churchyard, intersected with dykes and mounds and gates, with scattered cattle feeding on it, was the marches; and that the low leaden line beyond, was the river; and that the distant savage lair from which the wind was rushing, was the sea; and that the small bundle of shivers growing afraid of it all and beginning to cry, was Pip.
>
> 'Hold your noise!' cried a terrible voice, as a man started up from among the graves at the side of the church porch. 'Keep still, you little devil, or I'll cut your throat!'
>
> A fearful man, all in coarse grey, with a great iron on his leg. A man with no hat, and with broken shoes, and with an old rag tied round his head. A man who had been soaked in water, and smothered in mud, and lamed by stones, and cut by flints, and stung by nettles, and torn by briars; who limped, and shivered, and glared and growled; and whose teeth chattered in his head as he seized me by the chin.
>
> 'O! Don't cut my throat, sir', I pleaded in terror. 'Pray don't do it, sir.'
>
> 'Tell us your name!' said the man. 'Quick!'
>
> (Dickens [1860–1] 1965: 35–6)

This dramatic opening immediately raises two enigmas: who is this frightening figure and what affect will his possessive seizing hold of the orphaned child have upon Pip's subsequent life and expectations? The rest of the narrative is a hermeneutic network of false snares and positive clues as to the complete answers to these related mysteries. Although *Grace Notes* and *The Prime of Miss Jean Brodie* similarly set up mysteries in their opening pages, it is the stylistic difference of *Great Expectations* from the other two that is most striking. This is not primarily because it is a nineteenth-century text whereas they are contemporary novels. The difference resides in the fact that the prose of both *Grace Notes* and *The Prime of Miss Jean Brodie* is dominated by the metonymic principle of contiguity while the passage from *Great Expectations* is governed by what Jakobson terms the metaphoric principle of similarity. This is most easily recognised in the paragraph beginning 'A fearful man' which is wholly structured by similarities of rhythm, phrasing, syntax and the insistent repetition of the word 'man'. Yet the dominance of the metaphoric principle in the passage involves far more than formal patterns of similarity. It produces the symbolic system that will structure the whole narrative.

In his analysis of *Sarrasine*, Barthes points out that the symbolic field of a novel is frequently ordered by antithetical oppositions like good and evil. The extract from *Great Expectations* is structured upon very complex systems of interrelated antitheses. Perhaps most obviously, there is play upon the oppositions of the natural elements of wind, earth (the churchyard) and sea to the human world. Second, the reference to the churchyard and 'the small bundle of shivers' threatened with having his throat cut evokes a precarious antithesis of life to death. This antithesis associates with the notion of bestiality evoked by the 'savage lair of the wind' and the emphasised animal physicality and violence of the man's bodily state brought into an opposing relationship to the normal cultural connotations, even the biblical resonance, of 'man'. The same images symbolise the opposition of power to vulnerability or helplessness. Finally, there is the antithesis between the wildness and rushing energy of the unbound natural elements and the restriction and containment of human relationships of power and possession implied by the leg iron and the seizure of the child.

The stability of antithetical relationships is what holds the entire conceptual structure of any language in place. Meaning is a system of differences: the significance of the term 'evil', for example, derives from its binary opposition to 'good'. So, if the dense particularity of a realist text can be metaphorically reduced to simple antithetical terms, then the 'truth' of its resolution functions to affirm preconceived notions of the order of existence. It does not disturb or challenge conventional patterns of thinking. It is for this reason that Barthes argues that any mixing or joining of antithetical terms constitutes a transgression ([1973] 1990: 27). In *Sarrasine* the enigma that centres upon the character of that name, turns out to be a transgression. Sarrasine is a castrato and so erases the 'natural' opposition between male and female upon which so large a part of conventional social order is founded. The 'fearful man' of *Great Expectations* is also transgressive – not only as a criminal outlaw but semantically in exceeding the boundaries that define animal against human, nature against civilisation, and power against weakness. Jonathan Culler points out that in realist novels symbolism, associated primarily with the poetic functioning of language or Jakobson's metaphoric pole, tends to be recuperated to the metonymic mode of realism by means of contiguity (Culler 1975: 225). For example, in the extract from *Great Expectations*, the symbolism of graveyard and death and of elemental physical forces are 'naturalised' within the empirical effect by means of the proximity of cemetery and sea to Pip's home in the marsh country. This interdependence of metaphor and metonomy suggests a new way we might begin to understand and evaluate realism. At its most epistemologically challenging, realist writing produces a very complex balance between metaphor and metonymy, between the empirical effect and the truth effect, and this results in a radical testing of universal 'truths' against historical particularity in such a way that neither localism nor generalisation prevails.

THE CHARACTER EFFECT

The 'character effect' is probably, for many readers, the primary means of entry into the fictional world of a novel, or at least the main vehicle for effecting the willing suspension of disbelief. But how is the character effect achieved? Barthes ascribes this function to the semic code which he also calls the voice of the person. In the most general sense, a seme is simply a unit of meaning but Barthes emphasises their accretive capacity: 'When identical semes traverse the same proper name several times and appear to settle upon it, a character is created....The proper name acts as a magnetic field for the semes' ([1973] 1990: 67). The opening of George Eliot's novel, *Middlemarch* (1871) provides a clear illustration of this clustering of meaning around a name:

> Miss Brooke had that kind of beauty which seems to be thrown into
> relief by poor dress. Her hand and wrist were so finely formed that
> she could wear sleeves not less bare of style than those in which the
> Blessed Virgin appeared to Italian painters; and her profile as well as
> her stature and bearing seemed to gain the more dignity from her
> plain garments, which by the side of provincial fashion gave her the
> impressiveness of a fine quotation from the Bible.
>
> (Eliot [1871–2] 1994: 7)

Most competent readers can easily translate the semes, or units of
meaning, that constitute this passage according to notions of 'character'
that are already culturally familiar: physical beauty, dignity of
demeanour, a somewhat high-minded, even puritan, disregard for
ostentation of dress, the suggestion of moral seriousness connoted by
the religious associations. What the passage also lets us recognise is the
degree to which these character schemas that support the notion of
individuality are produced and circulated by various artistic and cultural conventions. Eliot is drawing here upon the long tradition of
painterly portraiture, upon religious models of character like 'the
Blessed Virgin', and perhaps even upon fairy tales of virtuous beauty
clothed in poor dress. To a remarkable extent, 'character', which is so
often taken as a privileged index of individual particularity, is largely the
location of a network of codes, and, of course, novels themselves not
only draw upon these cultural semes of personality but contribute powerfully to them. Barthes argues that what gives this semic convergence
'the illusion that the sum is supplemented by a precious remainder
(something like *individuality*...) is the Proper Name' ([1973] 1990:
191). For Barthes, it is pre-eminently the Proper Name that functions
ideologically to sustain belief in human identity as unique, coherent
and individual rather than as amorphous clusters of attributes. It is this
belief in the special particularity or individuality of each subject that
underlies humanism and bourgeois individualism. Thus, Barthes maintains 'all subversion...begins with the Proper Name' ([1973] 1990: 95).

However, Barthes almost certainly exaggerates the importance of the
Name in the constitution of individual fictional characters in realist
novels. No matter how complex or dense the semic convergence, it is
not wholly or mainly personality traits or attributes that produce the

character effect. Certainly semes do not create that sense of an inner consciousness or individual subjectivity that, in literary terms, has been most fully elaborated in novelistic prose. Elsewhere in *S/Z*, Barthes acknowledges that '*the character and the discourse are each other's accomplices*' (Barthes [1973] 1990: 178). A comparison of the character effect achieved by the opening description of Miss Brooke in *Middlemarch* with the effect produced by Miss Brodie's speech quickly indicates the importance of dialogue. Direct dialogue purporting to be a character's spoken words or sometimes the verbal articulation of their thoughts gives substance to the sense of an individual consciousness. Genette calls direct character dialogue 'objectivised speech' but he points out a paradoxical effect. The most 'realistic' dialogue is that which is rather banal and unmemorable. The more individualised and idiosyncratic a character's speech becomes, the more that character seems to be imitating and even caricaturing himself or herself. (Genette 1980: 185). This effect of self performance or self parody is clearly apparent in the case of Miss Brodie's speech pattern and functions in the text to make any sense of her identity strangely insubstantial and elusive. Thus dialogue is at once a primary means by which the ideological effect of a unique individuality is constructed but also deconstructed or at least discomforted in realist fiction.

The objectivised speech of characters is not the only way in which the effect of individual subjectivity or consciousness is produced. Other important techniques pertain to the division in narration summarised by Genette as 'who speaks' and 'who sees'. (Genette 1980: 186). Earlier critics termed these two aspects 'narrative point of view' and 'narrative voice'. Genette uses the term 'focalisation' to name the aspect of 'seeing', that is, the perspective from which characters and events are viewed (Genette 1980: 189). Consonance between narrative voice and narrative focalisation to provide detailed understanding of a character's psychology and subjective state of mind are a characteristic feature of nineteenth-century realist fiction. As typically used by realists like Balzac and George Eliot, such 'psycho-narration' can construct a very complex sense of a character's consciousness, and even illuminate elements of their psyche that would be unknowable to the person themselves. (I take the term 'psycho-narration' from Cohn 1978: 21–57, who provides a very detailed structural analysis of various forms of 'psycho-narration'.) Yet, for this very reason, consonant psycho-narration always maintains an evaluative distance from the individual consciousness or subjectivity that it describes and in so doing confirms for the reader a somewhat comforting and complacent sense of superior knowledge or wisdom to that of the character.

It is dissonance between narrative voice and focalisation that produces a more immediate or direct sense of a subjective consciousness. A complex form of such dissonance is that usually called **free indirect speech** in which the voice and focalisation of the narrator become, as it were, infected or invaded by the speech and perspective of a character. In the following passage from *Middlemarch*, in which Dorothea is courted by the rather elderly Mr Casaubon, the first two sentences are narrated and focalised by the impersonal narrator. Thereafter the passage undergoes a 'stylistic contagion' (Cohn 1978: 33) as the language, syntax and focalisation seem to merge with the fervour and rather naive idealism of Dorothea's consciousness:

> It was not many days before Mr Casaubon paid a morning visit, on which he was invited again for the following week to dine and stay the night. Thus Dorothea had three more conversations with him, and was convinced that her first impressions had been just. He was all she had at first imagined him to be: almost everything he had said seemed like a specimen from a mine, or the inscription on the door of a museum which might open on the treasures of past ages; and this trust in his mental wealth was all the deeper and more effective on her inclination because it was now obvious that his visits were made for her sake. This accomplished man condescended to think of a young girl, and take the pains to talk to her, not with absurd compliments, but with an appeal to her understanding, and sometimes with instructive correction. What delightful companionship!
>
> (Eliot [1871–2] 1994: 32)

The last exclamatory sentence here could easily be put straight into quotation marks as Dorothea's own emotional form of speech and eager perspective of an anticipated future. In the previous sentences the distinction between narrator and character is much more blurred. The somewhat exaggerated images of mine and museum as figures for

Casaubon's mind and heightened phrases like 'absurd compliment' seem expressions of Dorothea's emotional response and viewpoint, while the understanding that Dorothea's trust in her suitor's intellect is rendered 'all the deeper and more effective on her inclination' move closer to the more sober evaluative language and stance of the narrator. The grounding of free indirect speech in narrative voice and focalisation always maintains a potential position of greater knowledge and worldliness from which the stylistic contagion, that is the character's consciousness, can be evaluated. In this example from *Middlemarch*, the use of free indirect speech offers readers a sense of direct access to the heroine's subjective state of mind which provokes sympathetic understanding of her hopeful emotions but without loss of an objective perspective as to their possible dangers and limitations. Again in a case like this, one might argue that psychological realism is functioning here to confirm the availability of knowledge.

By contrast, the first person narration of *Great Expectations* sets up a dissonance between the focalisation of the adult narrator and the younger self as character in the story. The narrative voice and perspective of the adult Pip are frequently darkened by a brooding self-recrimination as to the moral weakness of his younger self. Yet the focalisation of the child Pip, as in the extract given above, produces a sense of him as largely a powerless victim of people and social forces over which he has little control. The total effect of this non-consonant focalisation is to raise radical questions as to the nature of subjectivity. Does self consist of an autonomous individuality responding with responsible free will to the promptings of conscience and rational judgement, or, is a self merely the product, 'the bundle of shivers', of coercive social pressures?

Modern novelists tend to follow Dickens's type of character effect; they abjure claims to superior knowledge of a character's psychology and subjectivity. In *Grace Notes*, third person narration is fused to the protagonist's, Catherine's, focalisation. The story opens with what could seem an over-detailed account of her early morning journey by bus to the airport until we realise that what is being conveyed is the consciousness of Catherine herself, desperately fixing her attention upon a trivial immediacy to keep her overwhelming feelings of grief blocked out. This narrative technique conveys the multiple, often contradictory levels of sensory, emotional and rational awareness that intermix to constitute subjectivite reality. It is the kind of many-layered complexity of perspective, voice, temporality and particularity that only novelistic prose, of all literary forms, achieves.

'Achieves' is the correct word here, facilitating an analytic, formalist understanding and evaluation of the complex artistry of realist writing. Too frequently, recent structural analyses of realism have resorted to reductive or suspicious terminology. Pointing out the means by which novels produce the effect of experiential particularity is understood by such critics in terms of unmasking duplicity. Typical of this kind of dismissive language is Genette's reference to the 'illusion of mimesis' and his implicit claim to be revealing the artifice that lies behind the trickery: 'The truth is that mimesis in words can only be mimesis of words' (Genette 1980: 164). The word 'only' in this sentence functions too easily to dismiss the impressive artistic techniques and formal arrangements and strategies outlined in this chapter and, of course, meticulously analysed by Genette himself. As I have also indicated throughout the chapter, these techniques do not function only in complicity with the existing status quo, they also discomfort prevailing assumptions, especially the tendency to naturalise and simplify historical particularity as universal, unchanging truth. In serious realist writing universality is always formally and rigorously tested against specificity.

6

THE READER EFFECT

In the previous chapter, I argued that we cannot do justice to the artistic achievement of literary realism or recognise its capacity to facilitate new ways of understanding our reality if we remain within a suspicious critical perspective that only perceives reality effects as illusions. Realist novels do not seek to trick their readers by 'illusion'; they do seek to give them pleasure from the recognition of verisimilitude. The empirical effect and the character effect are understood by the vast majority of ordinary readers as just that: an effect. When novels are praised as life-*like* this implicitly recognises they are not life. An effect cannot be identical to that which it aims to imitate. As we saw in Chapter 2, the language of critical detraction as applied to realism depends upon the construction of two kinds of implied readers: the naive readers who are duped by 'illusion' and the sceptically intelligent who know that it is *only* mimesis. One of the problems arising from this view is that it denies any means of evaluating or differentiating the vast, disparate range of writing that goes under the label of realism, some of which is undoubtedly thematically and formally conservative but some of which is certainly not. It also fails to take account of the complexity and variety of aesthetic, intellectual and pleasurable experiences that are subsumed under the term 'reading'. In this chapter, then, I want to begin to turn our attention to those aspects of reading that have been associated with realism as a genre from its beginnings: active enjoyment and knowledge production.

In referring to a 'reader effect', I am using the term in a somewhat different way to that implied by 'character effect' or 'empirical effect'. Clearly novel readers have an existence extrinsic to the text in a way that fictional characters and fictional worlds do not. Yet there is a sense in which literary works produce the kinds of readers they require. As we have seen, there was a symbiotic relationship between modernism as a practice of experimental writing and formalism as a innovative critical reading approach, both in American and in Russia. Modernist experimentalism and critical approval for writerly techniques of defamiliarisation radically altered the terms of literary evaluation, with the highest accolades going to those works perceived as challenging aesthetic conventions and defying accepted cultural norms. From the Russian Formalists to Adorno and the Frankfurt School and on to Roland Barthes and poststructuralist critics generally, a new critical tradition has developed which privileges writing that expresses a negative critique of prevailing cultural values. Alongside this shift in critical evaluation of literary art there has evolved a new perception of readers. Experimental writing, Barthes claims, produces the reader as 'no longer a consumer, but a producer of the text,' whereas conventional forms of writing, like realism, require only passive consumers of stories (Barthes [1973] 1990: 4) The elitism that underlies this division of readers emerges when Barthes writes of a moderately plural realism for which 'there exists an average appreciator' (Barthes [1973] 1990: 6). In addition to fostering a dismissive attitude towards the majority of readers, an aesthetics based purely upon negative critique has difficulty accounting for those positive values associated with art through many centuries and in many cultures from Aristotle to the present: affirmation, praise, learning, identification, enjoyment.

STANLEY FISH: INTERPRETIVE COMMUNITIES

American critic, Stanley Fish (1938–), a Renaissance scholar trained in the tradition of American New Criticism, has elaborated a more democratic and creative view of the reader. In reaction to New Criticism's insistence upon the self-contained autonomy of the text, Fish argues, that the meaning of a literary work and its formal structures are all produced by the interpretive assumptions and strategies that the reader brings to the text. For Fish, meaning and structure have no independent existence outside of the reading experience. The end point of this logic is Fish's insistence that it is the reader who 'writes' the text which only comes into being by means of the interpretive activity that is reading/writing. Indeed, even the recognition of a category of 'the literary' is a prior interpretive assumption upon which the whole critical enterprise depends for its *raison d'être*. Two questions are raised by Fish's empowerment of the reader as interpretive writer of the work: how, in that case, can even a relative critical consensus be achieved rather than critical anarchy and, conversely, why does the same reader produce different readings of a particular text at different times in her or his life? Fish meets these difficulties by elaborating a notion of 'interpretive communities': 'Interpretive communities are made up of those who share interpretive strategies not for reading (in the conventional sense) but for 'writing' texts, that is for constituting their properties and assigning their intentions' (Fish, 'Interpreting the *Variorum*', reprinted in Lodge 1988: 327). Thus, for example, readers who agree about the meaning of *Great Expectations* do so because they belong to the same interpretive community while the reader who changes her mind as to its form and values does so because he/she has adopted another interpretive affiliation.

Apart from Fish's insistence that an interpretive community produces or writes the text which has no other form of being, there does not seem anything very radical about this notion. However, it does suggest a way of accounting for the somewhat confused critical evaluation of realism. New Criticism, Russian Formalism and poststructuralism all produced new interpretive communities. The aesthetic values of a critical community largely determine those formal aspects of texts deemed noteworthy and to that extent, at least, they 'write' the work. By and large, the literary qualities favoured by New Critics, Russian Formalists and poststructuralists have been those associated with negative critique and self-reflexivity rather than verisimilitude. As a result, the interpretive strategies brought to bear on realist texts by these three communities have tended to perceive realism in terms of what it lacks rather than what it actually achieves. More recently, poststructuralist interpretive strategies have been applied positively to nineteenth-century realist novels and, behold, we discover that they too are ironic, self-reflexive and, structured by indeterminacy. Stanley Fish would claim that as members of a new interpretive community we are simply writing different novels from those that traditional critics wrote when they read *Bleak House*, or *Middlemarch* or *Cousin Bette*.

WOLFGANG ISER: THE IMPLIED READER AND WANDERING VIEWPOINT

The German reception theorist, Wolfgang Iser (1926–), was also, in the early part of his career, a practitioner of New Criticism but his understanding of the reader's role in producing the text is less radical than that of Stanley Fish. For Iser the relationship is more one of equal partnership: there is the objective existence of the literary work but this has to be actualised by the creative, subjective interaction of the reader. The literary form that most concerns Iser is the novel. The novel for Iser is somewhat like a schematic programme or skeleton outline that the reader completes through an 'act of concretization' (Iser 1980: 21). Yet Iser is not concerned with actual readers but with the implied reader imminent in the form of the text itself. He argues that, since texts only take on their potential reality through the act of being read, it follows that they must already contain 'the conditions that will allow their meaning to be assembled in the responsive mind of the recipient' (Iser 1980: 34). For Iser, then, in his theoretical considerations, the reader is the recipient implied by the interactive structures of the text. 'Thus the concept of the implied reader designates a network of response-inviting structures, which impel the reader to grasp the text.' (Iser 1980: 34) Among the most important of the novel's response-inviting strategies are the four main perspectives of narrator, characters, plot and the fictitious reader (Iser 1980: 35). None of these viewpoints are completely identical but, according to Iser, they provided differing starting points for the reader's creative process through the text. The role of the reader is to occupy the non-identical, shifting vantage points of the four textual perspectives 'that are geared to a prestructured activity and to fit the diverse perspectives into a gradually evolving pattern' (Iser 1980: 35).

Thus, taking *Great Expectations* as an example, the novel, in its first two pages, offers the reader at least four differing reading perspectives or starting points. There is that of the adult narrator sufficiently distanced from the immediacy of narrative events to describe his youthful self as 'the small bundle of shivers'. A second viewpoint is the character perspective of the child, Pip, and the urgency of his terror of the fearful man and sense of shivering powerlessness in the face of a hostile, violent world, both elemental and human. There is the third perspective of the convict, 'soaked', 'lamed', 'cut' and 'torn' who glares and growls with ferocity but also shivers like the child, who is a 'man' not a beast. Finally, I think we glimpse what can be understood as a fourth viewpoint, that of text or plot. It is conveyed pre-eminently by language associations and encompasses a larger perspective that any of the previous ones. What it expresses is a sense of 'that universal struggle' for the bare sufficiencies of life, warmth, food, shelter, love, in an order of existence that tilts towards death, suffering and want. Iser utilises the notion of 'wandering viewpoint' to suggest how the reader travels through the text inhabiting multiple perspective positions each of which influences, modifies and objectifies the others.

This creative activity of the reader in actualising the meaning imminent in the response-inviting structures and strategies of the text is relevant to the realist agenda of conveying knowledge about a non-textual reality. Iser rejects the poststructuralist view that texts can only refer to other texts, that there exists an unbridgeable gap between words and the world. Fiction and reality should not be placed in opposition, he argues, 'fiction is a means of telling us something about reality' (Iser 1980: 53). However, this should not be understood in terms of 'reflection' or 'imitation' of the reality conveyed because 'the conveyor [the text] cannot be identical to what is conveyed [reality]' (Iser 1980: 54). The relationship between novels and reality must be understood in terms of communication. Utilising the speech-act theory of J. L. Austin (1911–60), Iser suggests that a literary work should be thought of as an **illocutionary act**. In normal speech contexts illocutionary acts gain force only when speaker and recipient share the same conventions and procedures so that the recipient's response brings into being the speaker's intention or meaning. Magwitch's injunction to Pip, 'Hold your noise!' is an illocutionary act dependent upon Pip understanding what is required of him by the form and context of the utterance. Magwitch's words have no truth status as such but they connect to reality by their illocutionary force (which is irrespective of Magwitch's physical force) to produce a response.

Iser argues that novels are a special form of illocutionary act. They too organise and make use of cultural and linguistic conventions and procedures but within a literary text these conventions are separated from their normal and regulating context. Thus they become foregrounded for the reader as objects for conscious knowledge and evaluation. Iser calls these conventions the repertoire upon which the text calls and this repertoire constitutes a verbal territory shared by text and reader that initiates the act of communication that is reading. This act of communication tells us something new about reality because the literary text reorganises the familiar repertoire of social and cultural norms. As a result, readers are able 'to see what they cannot normally see in the ordinary process of day-to-day living' (Iser 1980: 74). In *Great Expectations* the fictional context of Magwitch's illocutionary command pushes into sharp focus the more usually veiled distribution of power between speaker and recipient that gives silencing injunctions their force. This knowledge about social reality is reinforced by Pip's utilisation of linguistic conventions of subordination such as begging, pleading, deference: 'Pray don't do it, sir.'

It seems rather more difficult to recognise what social and linguistic norms are being organised at the opening of *Middlemarch*. Yet perhaps we should understand it within the cultural and linguistic conventions of 'making an introduction'. This invokes all those literary traditions for starting a narrative but also all the social rituals of making a person known to new acquaintances: both of these conventions are performed with the expectation that they will illicit an appropriate response in recipients. As it turns out, *Middlemarch* is centrally concerned with rumour, prejudice, first impressions, and misunderstandings, so the illocutionary conventions associated with introductions constitute that aspect of the repertoire of the text that comes under closest scrutiny.

Although this approach to texts as illocutionary acts can clearly be productive it is open to the criticism that it fails to get beyond the limitation of negative critique. Literary value, for Iser, resides in the capacity of the work to recodify norms so as to question external reality, thereby allowing the reader to discover the motives and regulatory forces underlying the questions. The repertoire of the text 'reproduces the familiar, but strips it of its current validity.' (Iser 1980: 74). This may produce understanding of the power residing in communicative conventions but it does not offer much in the way of an approach to affirmative writing or the function of literature to provide enjoyment. However, Iser does see another positive epistemological outcome of the creative response the text provokes in the reader. In the process of reading a literary text, the reader must perforce enter into many perspectives or points of view, some of them quite unfamiliar, and this enables the reader to move out of that part of their self that has been determined by previous experience. They have to alienate part of themselves to accommodate what is new and other. The 'contrapuntally structured personality' produced by such reading results in an extended self-awareness in which 'a layer of the reader's personality is brought to light which had hitherto remained hidden in the shadows' (Iser 1980: 157). Reading statements like this in Iser's work, it is easy to forget that the reader here is only the implied reader; the reader Iser assembles from textual structures that seem to interpellate or call such an active reader/producer into existence. Understood from this perspective, the implied reader could equally be seen as the ideal of an enlightened, open-minded, European individual reader/critic imagined and interpellated by Iser himself that he then projects into texts. As Stanley Fish has commented, 'the adventures of the reader's "wandering viewpoint" – will be the products of an interpretive strategy that demands them' (Fish 1981: 7). Nevertheless, as we shall see in Part IV, Jürgen Habermas' (1929–) develops the notion of shifting perspective positions to set out a more general notion of knowledge as communicative discourse.

HANS ROBERT JAUSS: HORIZON OF EXPECTATION

Iser's colleague at Constance University, Hans Robert Jauss, was influenced by Russian Formalism rather than New Criticism. Jauss's concern with reception theory focuses upon the macro level of literary history. He argues that in order to properly understand the historical development of any literary genre it is necessary to recognise the dynamic 'interaction of author and public' (Jauss 1982: 15). To elucidate this interaction between writers and readers, Jauss turns to the Russian Formalists' concept of defamiliarisation, linking this to what he calls a 'horizon of expectation' (Jauss 1982: 23). This latter term is never precisely defined in his work but it seems to refer to an intersubjective set of expectations, cultural, aesthetic and social, that the generality of individuals bring to the reading or writing of any text. This would seem to bring him close to Fish's notion of an interpretive community. But Jauss theorises a triangular relationship between text, reader and world which allows a more critical and creative role to both texts and readers than is possible from within Fish's closed interpretive worlds. Jauss claims that defamiliarisation techniques in literary works challenge more that just the established artistic conventions familiar to their readers, they can produce a new evaluation of the everyday experience of life. Jauss writes, 'The social function of literature manifests itself in its genuine possibility only where the literary experience of the reader enters into the horizons of expectations of his lived praxis, reforms his understanding of the world, and thereby also has an effect on his social behaviour' (Jauss 1982: 39). He illustrates this claim by reference to Flaubert's novel, *Madame Bovary*: the new artistic devices of this work enabled it to 'radicalize or raise new questions of lived praxis' (Jauss 1982: 43). Thus Jauss stakes out a positive, even a utopian role for literary writing.

Nevertheless, Jauss came to realise that this perception remained caught up in the long negative critique deriving from the *l'art pour l'art* of mid-century aesthetic debates in France. Affirmative art cannot be accommodated within this critical evaluation. Jauss was dissatisfied by the concept of the reader as constituted in the tradition of negative critique. It only recognises two poles of reception for art. On the one hand, there is the conception of an élite group of readers and critics able to respond to the alienating form of avant-garde art. On the other hand, there is the vast majority of people who are relegated to the role of passive consumers of banal conventions. Such a puritan aesthetics leaves a huge range of art work and response to it unaccounted for between the two poles of its extremes. Jauss points out that this high value accorded the new is a very recent shift in artistic judgement and one which coincides with the mass commodification of art products in the nineteenth-century. Jauss wants to find a way of doing justice to the neglected functions of art by returning to a much older recognition of the 'primary unity of understanding enjoyment and enjoying understanding' (cited in Holub 1984: 75). This looks back to Aristotle's non-separation of knowledge and pleasure. In *Poetics*, Aristotle gives imitation a central role in learning, arguing that it is the imitative capacity above all that ensures human's superiority to brutes: 'it is natural for all human beings to delight in works of imitation' (Aristotle 1963: 8). This delight is evident even when the object of imitation is itself offensive, as with the form of a dead body and this is because delight in imitation is directly related to the enjoyment that comes from acquiring knowledge: 'To be learning something is the greatest of pleasures not only to philosophers but also to the rest of mankind....The reason for the pleasure derived from looking at pictures is that one is at the same time learning – gathering the meaning of things' (Aristotle 1963: 8).

'Gathering the meaning of things' as an expression of the cognitive function of art by no means has to depend upon a reflectionist or **positivism** correspondence view of either literary work or knowledge. Certainly Jauss is not primarily concerned with artistic verisimilitude. He looks back to Leonardo da Vinci as an ideal of an artist whose formal practice encompassed a pursuit of knowledge. His poetic praxis constitutes 'cognition dependent on what one can do, on a form of action that tries and tests so that understanding and producing can become one' (cited in Holub 1984: 75). Jauss understands the interrelated cognitive, communicative and enjoyment functions of art in terms of three traditional critical categories: poetics, aesthetics and catharsis. He reconceptualises these within the context of a mass capitalist mode of production to emphasise their creative potential for knowledge generation allied to pleasure.

Poetics, as usually understood, refers to the activity and pleasure to be derived from an ability to produce an art object. In the ancient world this activity was understood in terms of imitation of transcendent Forms. By the Renaissance this association of knowledge, creative practice and perfection had become located in the individual artist's skill and vision. With the advent of mass industrialisation, aesthetic activity remained the only form of non-alienated creative production. In this century, as art work has come to be characterised by indeterminacy and ambiguity, the reader too has been brought within the ambit of poetics in its extended meaning as creative praxis that evokes knowledge as enjoyment of self-discovered ability.

Jauss associates aesthetics, the reception side of artistic activity, with the positive potential for community. As opposed to the growing alienation of modern atomistic social existence, art can provide a space for the experience of communicative bonds through the practices of shared knowledge and enjoyment. Finally, with his third term, catharsis, Jauss considers ways in which identification functions as an important element in artistic reception. He rejects the model of two extremes of either avant-garde producer or passive consumer. Instead he suggests five interactive modes of identification that characterise the reader's receptive position. All of these identifying positions available to the recipient as reader or audience involve forms of knowledge as enjoyable praxis and, of course, any one literary work can offer the reader a shifting range of possible identifications.

Jauss's ideas, like these on identification, often seem schematic rather than fully developed. Looking at a passage like that from *The Prime of Miss Jean Brodie*, for example, the complex, shifting identifications of the reader seem easier to analyse by means of Iser's notion of wandering viewpoint than by five separate modes of identification. In turning to the work of Jauss I have undoubtedly moved beyond the range of criticism that can be called formalist in that its primary concern is with qualities imminent in the text. Nevertheless, Jauss, coming from the tradition of Russian Formalism, is helpful for a reconsideration and re-evaluation of realism because of his central concern to reconnect literature to knowledge production and to enjoyment. These have been two of the persistent claims underpinning any privileged or continuing regard for realist writing. Jauss's work challenges an over-simple positivist view of knowledge or realism as a kind of hollow transmission tube that aims to convey an accurate unmediated reality. He reminds us that knowledge can also be a form of creative praxis associated with pleasure. Together with Wolfgang Iser he urges us to think of novels and reading as very complex communicative acts. In opposition to the more nihilistic, anti-humanist, anti-realist theories of writing, he affirms the cognitive and communal functions of art. In the final chapter I shall argue for a defining association of realist writing with knowledge, community, pleasure and justice.

IV

REALISM AND
KNOWLEDGE
A Utopian Project?

7

REALISM AND THE CRISIS
OF KNOWLEDGE

'Knowledge is power' was widely proclaimed, during the nineteenth
century, as the aspirational slogan of the radical press and working-class
political and educational movements. In using it, political radicals and
working people were consciously aligning themselves with the tradition
of eighteenth-century Enlightenment which linked the universal ideals
of freedom, equality and justice with the pursuit of progress and rational knowledge. By and large, the realist writers of the nineteenth century also associated their literary endeavours with Enlightenment ideals
as against what were seen as the reactionary politics and prejudices of
the *ancien régime*. Dickens, Hardy, Balzac and Zola used their novels to
attack arbitrary authority, corrupt officialdom, the abuse of justice and
to highlight the oppression and suffering of those victimised. Like
Aristotle, they believed that mimesis, representation of the world, could
function, without contradiction, as a source of both popular pleasure
and progressive knowledge and politics. Early twentieth-century
Marxist and humanist critics of realism like Lukács and Auerbach also
evaluated the genre within this general Enlightenment perspective.
Lukács argues that realism is defined by its profound historical imagination that offers unique insights into the underlying forces shaping alike
the social formation and individual types. Auerbach aligned a realist
project, stretching from Homer to Woolf, with the expansion of democratic ideals. For Auerbach, realism is defined as the first serious artistic
representation of everyday life.

At the beginning of Chapter 1, I claimed that questions of knowledge are inseparable from an understanding of realism as a representational form. It is my aim in these final chapters to argue for a positive understanding of realism which I shall define as a genre based upon an implicit communicative contract with the reader that there exists an independent, extra-textual real-world and that knowledge of this real-world can be produced and shared. This performative investment in the possibility of communicative knowledge undoubtedly joins realism, whatever its subject matter, to the emancipatory project of the Enlightenment. The capacity for intersubjective communication is the prerequisite for community and community is the necessary location of all particular individual civic and political rights and responsibilities. Sharable knowledge about the conditions of existence of embodied human creatures in the geographical world constitutes the material basis from which universal claims of justice and well-being must spring. Yet, the literary field in which late twentieth-century and early twenty-first century writing is produced is very different from that in which French and English nineteenth-century realists operated. In the first place, democratic institutions and scientific advances have frequently disappointed any optimistic hope of human advance. This in turn has led to what we might see as a crisis in the very possibility of knowledge. Yet, as Brecht retorted to Lukács against any over-narrow definition of realism: 'If we wish to have a living and combative literature, which is fully engaged with reality and fully grasps reality, a truly popular literature, we must keep step with the rapid development of reality' (Brecht 1977: 85). Brecht's sense of the genre as always in process and transition dismantles that unhelpful binary opposition that misrepresents realism as the conservative other to radical avant-garde experimentalism. Within the present literary and theoretical field, however, a coherent defence of realism must start from an understanding of the crisis of knowledge which has led to such widespread anti-realism in current critical, cultural and philosophical thought.

As outlined in Chapter 1, the Enlightenment project, centred upon rationality, came, during the twentieth century, to be viewed in a pessimistic light. 'Knowledge is power' is now understood, within much cultural theory, as expressing a more sinister truth. In *Dialectic of Enlightenment* (1944), Adorno and Horkheimer turned Enlightenment's rational critique against reason itself. They argued that the conception and constitution of knowledge during the Enlightenment was overly concerned with control and mastery. Rationality, they claimed, was conceived exclusively in terms of individual consciousness, of a human subject who observes the external world as passive object to be understood and systematised. This perception of knowledge is often referred to as subject-centred; it is criticised as self-assertively individualistic and as aggrandising the power of reason to order and subordinate the world in the pursuit of material and economic 'progress'.

In addition to this influential critique initiated by the Frankfurt School, the logical trajectory of Enlightenment empiricism itself was running into trouble by the early decades of the twentieth century. Seventeenth- and eighteenth-century empiricism, as elaborated by the philosophers John Locke (1632–1704) and David Hume (1711–76), placed human experience and observation of the material world at the centre of knowledge acquisition as part of their exclusion of religious and metaphysical beliefs from the domain of rational understanding. The increasing success of the empirical and experimental sciences during the eighteenth and nineteenth centuries appeared to confirm the truth and validity claims of this secular perception of knowledge. Yet empiricism is based upon a logical contradiction that eventually undermines the notion of truth upon which objective scientific knowledge rests.

LOGICAL POSITIVISM AND THE VERIFIABILITY PRINCIPLE

Taken in one direction, the empirical project leads to logical positivism, a development of the mathematical philosophy of Bertrand Russell (1872–1970) and the early work of Ludwig Wittgenstein (1889–1951) and expounded in the Vienna Circle during the 1920s and 1930s. It was logical positivism in particular that Adorno and the Frankfurt School took as the paradigm of a narrow systematising form of reason. Logical positivists severely restrict notions of truth to only those matters of fact that can be verified by empirical observation or experiment. The ideal of truth for which they aim is mathematical certainty. Any thing that cannot be verified, and that would include all universal ideals like justice, equality and freedom, cannot be deemed either true or false and hence cannot be recognised as meaningful objects of knowledge. This 'verifiability principle' produces a notion of truth that constitutes an ideal of exact correspondence between a propositional statement about a piece of the world and that actual piece of material existence. The definition of truth as what is verifiable lends itself to a pictorial analogy in which a statement or proposition is visualised as an image or picture which exactly copies or corresponds to an objective physical reality. A simple example would be the proposition 'The Houses of Parliament are situated on the bank of the Thames at Westminster'.

It is frequently this rather restricted view of verifiable truth, largely formalised in the early twentieth century, that is projected backwards onto fictional realism in the kinds of critique that accuse realists of claiming to offer readers a true picture of the world or a one-to-one correspondence between their writing and social reality. As we saw in Part II, nineteenth-century realists were very far from making such absolutist claims. One of the great formal achievements of nineteenth-century fiction was its experimental development of shifting and multiple focalisations and perspectives. Ultimately, logical positivism has proved to be somewhat a dead end. Too many domains of human experience and values have to be excluded from the realm of knowledge and truth according to the verifiability principle. In addition, subatomic particle science has moved well beyond the range of empirical validity testing that logical positivism defined as the only basis of scientific truth. What logical positivism undoubtedly brought into focus is the extreme difficulty of grounding truth claims upon any wholly objective and absolute foundation.

RELATIVE TRUTHS AND INCOMMENSURATE WORLDS

The second logical path from nineteenth-century empirical sciences leads to the opposite extreme from an over-restriction on what can be deemed truth, but it equally contributes to the crisis of knowledge. If empirical knowledge derives from the observation of material reality then, it can be argued, its truth is dependent upon the subjective response of the observer: truth therefore has to be recognised as relative and multiple. This line of thought was much influenced by the later work of Ludwig Wittgenstein on language in which he rejected his earlier concern with logical truth. Wittgenstein suggested that meaning should be understood in terms of 'language games' in which, analogously to other games like chess, it is rule-governed practice that produces significance. The 'meaning' of the bishop's move is only understandable or coherent in terms of the rules that govern chess. Similarly, Wittgenstein says 'The use of a word *in practice* is its meaning' (Wittgenstein [1933–35] 1972: 69). Meaning thus understood becomes enclosed within the set of rules that demarcate separate language games. Within the scientific field, development of subatomic physics seems to provide analogous evidence of separate meaning systems in which the rules of one **conceptual scheme** are nontransferable or incommensurate to the other. The system of knowledge that governs Newtonian science is completely irrelevant when it come to explaining the existence and form of subatomic particles. The logic and knowledge of one world does not transfer to the other. This perception of a complete shift of conceptual scheme as a means of understanding physical reality radically questions the Enlightenment sense of scientific reason as a continuous process of expanding knowledge. In place of that progressive history, philosopher of science, Thomas Kuhn (1922–96), set out a very influential theory claiming that science must be understood in terms of radical paradigm changes in which one systematic way of knowing the world is wholly replaced by another (Kuhn 1970).

This sense of **incommensurate worlds** and relative realities was augmented by the 'linguistic turn' Saussure's work gave to twentieth-century western thought. Language itself was to be understood as a self-contained system that produced meaning by means of its own structural rules. This insight led inevitably to the central thesis of the 'cultural turn': language does not reflect external reality, rather it constructs the order that we perceive as our world. As we saw in Chapter 2, sceptical, anti-realism became the new orthodoxy within poststructural and postmodern cultural theory from around the 1960s onwards. Within this purview, claims of universal truth and principle are regarded as mistaken, misleading and politically suspect. The claims of disinterested objectivity and generality put forward in many fields of scientific and cultural knowledge have been shown to be the relative and self-interested constructions of western masculine forms of understanding. Realist novels have been included in this critique in so far as they appear to offer their individualist, frequently bourgeois protagonists as examples of a universal human nature. In opposition to all such bogus, aggrandising, and imperialist universalism, poststructuralists and multiculturalists insist upon the irremediably local nature of truth, validity and knowledge; they affirm the irreducible difference of a plurality of incommensurate worlds. In contrast to the Enlightenment aim of totalising knowledge, postmodern theory has tended to focus upon the individual physical body as the most local site of cultural production.

MICHEL FOUCAULT AND KNOWLEDGE AS POWER

It was the French poststructural historian, Michel Foucault (1926–1984), however, who launched the most direct attack upon the twinned ideals of knowledge and progress. Foucault rejects both the Enlightenment sense of history as a continuous temporal progression and the ideal of science as participating in the historical narrative of human improvement. Foucault's **New Historicism** dissolves history into a series of discontinuous '**epistemes**' (Foucault 1961 and 1969). By the term episteme, Foucault conceptualises a total way of perceiving the world, a totalised order of things, that determines everything that can be known and said during each particular historical moment. An epistemic order of reality is produced and sustained by an interconnected network of discursive practices: religious, political, literary, scientific and everyday. These discursive formations are, like the epistemes they produce, discontinuous and incommensurate. What can be thought and said within one particular epoch is inconceivable to the understood order of things within another.

Foucault's main object of scholarly interest is the modern age or episteme that comes into being around the eighteenth century and is closely associated by him with the rise of the human sciences. The new interest in the scientific treatment of the insane from the end of the seventeenth century onwards is understood by Foucault not as a sign of progressive rational enlightenment but as the inception of a wholly new form of disciplinary social order based upon regulatory reason (Foucault 1963). Foucault sees the birth of medical and social institutions like the clinic, the prison, the school, the barracks, the hospital as the materi-alised mechanisms and practices of a will to power that masks itself as knowledge. All of these institutions are based upon a regime of surveil-lance and observation that positions any persons suspected of potential deviance within a field of relentless watchfulness. Those who are sub-jected to this all-seeing gaze come to internalise surveillance, disciplin-ing themselves into conformity with regulatory social and moral norms. Thus, for Foucault the modern age is carceral, or imprisoning, in its basic social structure: the entire population is caught within capillary mechanisms that intervene in the minutiae of every action and thought. These regulatory mechanisms of disciplinary knowledge are targeted upon the individual body which is discursively produced as the always dangerous location of potential deviancy: sexual, vagrant, disorderly, rowdy, insane, criminal (Foucault 1976).

Foucault has been criticised for his pervasive, unanchored notion of power which tends to represent it as totalising and omnipresent in every sphere of human life. Nevertheless, New Historicism has pro-duced some of the most rigorous and insightful of recent critical approaches to nineteenth-century realist writing. In this body of work novels are read as actively participating within the wider **discursive networks** that constitute nineteenth-century epistemic reality. So, for example, critic Mary Poovey reads Dickens's *Our Mutual Friend* (1864–5) as part of proliferating discourses concerned to represent speculative capitalism as an impersonal, amoral order beyond the remit of moral judgement (Poovey 1995: 155–81). D. A. Miller analyses *Bleak House* (1852–3) to demonstrate the way the text is complicit with the expanding disciplinary mechanisms of moral conformity in Victorian public and private spheres (Miller 1988: 58–106). Catherine Gallagher, in *The Industrial Reformation of English Fiction* (1985), shows the way the realist novel itself was transformed by its participa-tion in the new discourse of industrialism that emerged in the early decades of the nineteenth century. John Plotz has recently made a sim-ilar argument for the impact of Chartism and the nineteenth-century crowd upon literary forms. With variations of emphasis and approach, all of these New Historicist critics concur with Poovey's claim that critical analysis and historical studies are 'facets of a single enterprise' (Poovey 1995: 1).

This approach to realist fiction has been impressively fruitful in its ability to reconnect literary texts to the worlds they purport to represent yet without resorting to reflectionist claims that novels are offering a true or accurate picture of their times. New Historicist studies have illuminated the very complex ways in which realist writing, like that of all other discourses and genres, is governed and organised by those ideological struggles that are constitutive of the social realities at the moment of production. The analysis of realist texts from this perspective often facilitates recognition of the tensions and contradictions located at the point of competing value systems. Gallagher, for instance, indicates the way traditional paternalism co-existed in an uneasy relationship with the new market values of political economy within early representations of industrial conflict, as in Elizabeth Gaskell's novel, *Mary Barton* (1848), for example. The limitation of much New Historicism is that it remains largely a negative critique unable to account for the pleasures of a text or acknowledge a text's capacity to generate its own forms of knowledge. New Historicist readings tend to confirm the complicity of realism with repressive ideological discourses. Even when New Historicists highlight the contradictions and tensions between competing discursive structures in a text or moments of textual transgression, the ultimate conclusion of analysis is usually to demonstrate that, as Gallagher says, 'formal and ideological transgressions are elicited by and recontained within the logic of larger historical discourses' (Gallagher 1985: xiii–xvi).

As an example of New Historicist practice let us look briefly at D. A. Miller's reading of *Bleak House*. He suggests that Dickens's representation of the Court of Chancery with its pervasive, labyrinthine powers and interminable and obscurantist legal practices can be understood mimetically as an image of the developing Victorian state bureaucracy that would spread regulatory tentacles into all areas of social and private life (Miller 1988). Miller argues that the novel is structured around two opposing domains: there is the public carceral domain of entanglement within the institution of law and there is the domain of freedom and privacy located in the family. As well as representing the newly expanding bureaucratic state power by means of Chancery, *Bleak House* also offers its readers the new figure of the detective policeman in the character of Mr Bucket. In the course of his various investigations, Mr

Bucket continuously traverses the boundaries between institutional space and family privacy. He appears to protect the family and invade it. Thus, even as the novel holds out to its readers the promised ideal of family sanctity, it suggests the family's porosity and openness to scrutiny from outside. What the novel teaches its readers is that to maintain its right to privacy, the family must continually police itself.

Miller further suggests that the very form of the novel, particularly its length and complexity collude with these ideological effects. The complicated, intertwined strands of the story, the sustained mysteries of the plot, and the duration of reading, all work together, Miller argues to establish the text as 'a little bureaucracy of its own', so that despite the thematic satire upon the Court of Chancery, '*Bleak House* is profoundly concerned to train us…in the sensibility for inhabiting the new bureau-cratic, administrative structures' (Miller 1988: 88, 89).

This brief summary does not do justice to Miller's lengthy, subtle and complex essay on *Bleak House,* the reading of which could itself be seen as a disciplinary practice! What does become apparent is the ten-dency within New Historicism, to render power monolithic. In Miller's reading uneven historical developments and different degrees of social coercion are levelled into the uniform oppression of a totalised disci-plinary regime. Miller's discussion of *Bleak House* is part of his larger study of nineteenth-century novels entitled *The Novel and the Police* (1988). The work elaborates a parity between the ideological function-ing of police powers, newly established in the nineteenth century, and those of realist fiction. In doing so, it erases all distinction between the callous brutality meted out by the state to those without family or homes and the tactfulness with which authority approaches those shel-tered by domestic privacy. To suggest that novel readers are subjected to similar disciplinary mechanisms as are social outcasts and vagrants is to lose sight of the more important differences.

A much more nuanced recent study deriving from a New Historicist perspective, Nancy Armstrong's *Realism in the Age of Photograph* (1999), shifts critical attention from the entanglement of realist novels in ideo-logical discourses to their interaction with visual codes of reality. This usefully reminds us of the strong element of pictorialism that distin-guishes literary realism as a genre and that has tended to be overlooked in the current theoretical concern with the constitutive function of language. Nineteenth-century realism and photography developed at approximately the same time. To some extent this may account for the easy assumption that in producing a pictorial effect realist novels offer a kind of verbal snapshot. As I stressed in the Introduction, there can be no simple equation of the verbal and the visual. Yet Armstrong suggests that there is an important connection between the two major realist forms of the novel and photography. Armstrong argues that, from around the mid-nineteenth century, fiction and photography collaborated to provide the literate public with a proliferating supply of images and a set of unstated rules for interpreting them (Armstrong 1999: 3). Photography found a ready public among the Victorians and taking photographs soon became a widespread activity, enthusiastically patronised by Queen Victoria herself. (See Dimond and Taylor 1987; Homans 1995.) For both consumers and producers, photography was regarded as a technology of science and knowledge rather than an art form. Photographs promised more accuracy than any previous visual illustration, they appeared less influenced by subjective fallibilities of the observer, and they opened up new regions of reality to visual scrutiny: city slums, panoramic overviews, exotic racial peoples and landscapes, mug shots of criminals and the insane. Armstrong argues that despite the rapid proliferation in the quantity of visual images for consumption from the mid-century onwards, there was not a concomitant expansion in the variety. Increasingly, photography established and adhered to generic protocols for classifying, posing, shooting and naming its subject matter (Armstrong 1999: 21). For example, urban space was repeatedly photographed according to three distinct territorial models: the decaying slum, the dynamic flow of business and traffic through arterial networks of streets, the privacy of the suburban home. Photographs of people similarly utilised quite distinct poses for portraits to suggest the interiority of a cultured sensibility, the blank full-faced mug shot of the deviant or criminal, the abject posture to indicate the racial degeneracy of 'natives'. Armstrong argues that as a result of this continuous repetition of predictable visual images 'an entire epistemology of knowing imperceptibly installed itself in readers' imaginations along with the images that allowed them to identify virtually anything that either had been or could be rendered as a photograph' (Armstrong 1999: 21).

This process of accumulation produced a visual order of things that acquired the truth-status of an order of actual reality. Novels that wanted to be accessible and convincing to a mass readership henceforward had to conform to the visual protocols that regulated how the world was seen. Armstrong argues that works of realism 'do not attempt to 'reflect' an extratextual reality', instead they 'render legible in visual terms...the city, the Celtic fringe, the colonies, territories attractive to the camera as well' (Armstrong 1999: 11). When *Bleak House* 'refers to the street people and dilapidated tenements of nineteenth-century London, the novel is actually referring to what either was or would become a photographic commonplace' (Armstrong 1999: 5).

Armstrong sees the impatience of Modernist writers with what they condemn as realism's over-concern with the appearance of things as conceptually mistaken. She insists that there is no truth or knowledge to be discovered about some more authentic realm of reality beyond images. There is always only an order of things which produces and sustains the forms of 'knowledge' conceivable. There is nothing beyond representation. Armstrong defines realism as 'any representation that establishes and maintains the...social categories that an individual could or could not actually occupy' (Armstrong 1999: 168). It will be my aim in the final chapter to argue that realism can and does rationally refer to a material domain beyond representation and can and does communicate knowledge of that extra-textual reality. In pursuit of that aim it will be useful to follow up the valuable insight offered by Armstrong that novels are profoundly concerned with the political organisation of geographical space.

8

REALISM AND OTHER POSSIBLE WORLDS

The pictorial or visual aspect of realism is perhaps the characteristic of the genre that lends most credence to the view that such writing fosters an illusion of offering an accurate correspondence of a material reality beyond the text. From an anti-realist, postmodern position this is either naive or dishonest; unmediated knowledge of the world is not available, discourses or textuality constitute the only sense of reality we can possibly perceive and know. Yet literary realism, as I have defined it, is distinguished by its implicit contract with the reader that it does refer in some way to a world beyond the text. For that reason, to defend realist writing from the charge of naivety or bad faith, I must turn in this final chapter to the wider philosophical arguments brought more generally against current anti-realist theories of knowledge, truth and the world. Although most of these projects to rehabilitate realism are not concerned specifically with literary realism, I will try as far as possible to keep that relevance to the fore.

REALISM AND THE POLITICS OF SPACE

It will be helpful to begin by emphasising that visualising aspect of realism which perhaps elicits most immediate pleasure in readers: its world-representing capacity. Thomas Hardy immediately comes to mind as a writer whose work is shaped by a geographical imagination as well as a historical understanding. In Chapter 4, I discussed the historical implications of the episode in *Tess of the D'Urbervilles* where Tess and Angel Clare deliver milk to the isolated country railway station for transportation to London consumers. The geographical perception that underpins the representation of agricultural work in the novel is equally complex and impressive. Tess's only period of well-being in the story is the summer time she spends at the dairy. Yet Hardy does not represent Talbothays farm in terms of a utopian space. The dairy is progressively modern, producing milk for urban mass consumption. It can only do this because of its geographical proximity to a new railway connection and because it is situated in the water-meadows of the fertile Var Vale with the capacity to graze a large herd of dairy cows: 'there are nearly a hundred milchers under Crick's management' (Hardy [1891] 1988: 113). The word 'management' notes the market orientation of this enterprise. The dairy's size and up-to-datedness make it the sensible choice for Clare's agricultural apprenticeship before going out to South America as a colonial farmer. Clare's possession of abstract scientific knowledge as well as practical experience is a form of capital that he accumulates from the developed agricultural world of Europe. It allows him to colonise the undeveloped geography of South America where land was offered 'on exceptionally advantageous terms' (Hardy [1891] 1988: 355). Tess has superior practical skills but lacks the capital of scientific knowledge and for her the only means of livelihood is gruelling winter work within the harsh terrain of Flintcomb-Ash where the 'stubborn soil...showed plainly enough that the kind of labour in demand here was of the roughest kind' (Hardy [1891] 1988: 274). In the bleak upland geography of this location modernisation was not an option. The winter crop of swedes had to be manually forked from the stony soil as food for livestock. Hardy thus represents Tess at the nexus of interconnecting forces of differently valued knowledge, physical geography, agricultural economics, class, communication infrastructure, and colonial expansion. His geographical imagination grasps the spatial relationship between those local, national and global forces and the individual physical body of a female land-worker.

In *The Shipping News* (1993) by Annie Proulx (1935–), a whole community is represented in which all individual lives and social relations are shaped by the extremes of geography and weather on the Newfoundland arctic coast. There is, in the text, a historical understanding also of the international, national and local forces of change upon the community, but it is undoubtedly the particularity of a starkly unfamiliar geography and its pattern of life that imposes itself upon the reader's imagination. There is no way for the majority of readers responding to the realist force of the writing to verify the accuracy with which Proulx represents the strange social and physical world of the story. In any case, she explicitly disclaims factuality: 'The Newfoundland in this book, though salted with grains of truth, is a island of invention' (Proulx 1993: author's disclaimer). Indeed, this novel could be read as a fairy story told in an intensely realist mode. What might be called the world-disclosing knowledge that the realism of this text enforces is not that of accurate documentation. It is the knowledge of the possibility of other possible real-worlds to the one that we inhabit and are habituated to. As such it extends the horizons of the patterns of existence that we can imagine for embodied beings. It suggests to us that things do not of necessity have to be as we currently know them.

In *Spaces of Hope* (2000), geographer David Harvey argues that a more complex geographical understanding is required to encompass the spatial politics and forces of the modern world. He writes, 'Human beings have typically produced a nested hierarchy of spatial scales within which to organize their activities and understand their world...matters look differently when analyzed at global, continental, national, regional, local, or household/personal scales.' (Harvey 2000: 75) We not only need to develop this awareness of different spatial scales and their different realities, Harvey says, we also need to comprehend the forces that continually create, sustain, decompose and reconstruct spatial domains. Yet, Harvey is critical of postmodern representations of a globalised world that emphasise only continuous flux, shifting identities and ubiquitous unlocated power. A politics of justice he argues needs a firmer grounding of the material conditions of peoples' existence in a concrete historical and geographical world. Of all literary forms the realist novel is most suited to facilitate this kind of geographical understanding. It typically grasps the individual not just as an identity located in space but as 'a juncture in a relational system without determined boundaries in time and space' (Harvey 1996: 167).

In his essay 'Forms of Time and of the Chronotope in the Novel', Mikhail Bakhtin uses the term 'chronotope' to refer to the perception of human existence as a temporal/spatial juncture and he credits the realist novel with developing this essentially modern way of understanding and representing human life (1981: 84–258). Seen in this way, the individual, as the small spatial unit that comprises physical embodiment, has to be thought of as the location of the particular and the universal. As with Hardy's fictional representation of Tess, individual human beings participate in all stages of the hierarchy of geographical scales from global, to national, to local, right down to the physical body. For this reason, postmodern rejection of universalism for localism is inadequate. What is required is a way of understanding the particular in its inseparable dynamic connection with the universal or general. As I suggested in Chapter 5, novelistic language has developed various strategies and resources that facilitate the translation of the particular experience of protagonists into the realm of universal realities. In the episode where Tess takes milk to the London train, Hardy uses the imagery of the aged holly tree to imaginatively translate the modern experience of Tess at the cusp of two historical worlds into an infinitely longer temporal perspective encompassing the long process of historical change that has caught up and shaped individual human lives throughout time. This notion of translation between the particular and the universal, between different realms of historical experience, different geographical scales, different languages and worlds is central to what follows.

Postmodern literary and cultural criticism, especially that informed by postcolonial thinking, stresses the incommensurability of other worlds, the localism of known realities. It is argued that without a degree of common cultural roots in a community and place, experience and knowledge is incommunicable. Meanings can only be shared within autonomous 'interpretive communities'. The subjective thoughts and feelings of an illiterate Indian female bonded labourer, for example, are held to be inaccessible to a western woman with the privileges of education, sanitation, and professional career. It is claimed that to speak for the wretched of the earth is to enact another form of colonisation upon them. Such arguments are politically sobering and morally powerful. Yet, the bonded Indian labourer and the educated Western academic do not live in hermetically sealed different worlds. Their lives are

multiply interlinked by a powerful communicative currency that translates effortlessly across all geographical and linguistic boundaries:
money. If we are even to hope that it may be possible to produce a
world of greater justice and less exploitation we need to find other
forms of communicative currency that can traverse spatial scales of
global, national and local citizenship; forms that can draw strength
from being embedded in the particularity of individual existence but
translate into wider fields of meaning. Judging from the world-wide
ubiquity of narrative and the universal pleasures of story-telling, it
might be that fiction is one such currency. The word 'fiction' also draws
attention to another way of thinking about knowledge in contrast to a
strictly empirical epistemology based upon observation of the existing
material world. There is knowledge as creative activity, knowledge that
perceives connections and similarities where none have previously been
recognised, knowledge that projects possible worlds rather than measur-
ing the world as we presently have it.

But is such thinking utopian? Given the crisis of knowledge outlined
in the previous chapter and the persuasive anti-realist and anti-humanist theories that currently dominate western intellectual thought, is
knowledge of other worlds and communication between them possible?
Are universal notions of justice and well-being incoherent?
Wittgenstein's early work exerted a strong influence on logical positivism with its verifiability principle and severe curtailment of what
could properly count as truth; his later concept of language games fed
into the influential relativism of philosophers like Richard Rorty (Rorty
1991, vol. 1, contains a discussion of Donald Davidson, whose work is
outlined in this chapter. Also relevant is Rorty 1991, vol. 2, which
includes commentary on Lyotard, Habermas and Christopher Norris.)
Yet Wittgenstein's later writings also point to a way out from both of
these epistemological end points. Wittgenstein came to dismiss correspondence notions of truth that look for an exact match between a
statement about a state of affairs and the verifiable empirical observation of that actual state. 'A picture held us captive' is how he came to
describe that very limited view of realist representation (Wittgenstein
[1945–49] 1972: 48e). Instead of this picture or correspondence notion
of how words convey truths about the world he suggests that to imagine
a language is also to conceive of a form of social life (Wittgenstein

[1945–49] 1972: 8e). He asks, 'Suppose you came as an explorer into an unknown country with a language quite strange to you? In what circumstances would you say that the people there gave orders, understood them...and so on?' (Wittgenstein [1945–49] 1972: 82e) The answer he gives to this question is, 'The common behaviour of mankind is the system of reference by means of which we interpret an unknown language' (Wittgenstein [1945–49] 1972: 82e).

DONALD DAVIDSON AND INTERPRETIVE CHARITY

The issue of translation that Wittgenstein raises here is taken up by the American philosopher Donald Davidson to become the central thrust of his critique of all anti-realist arguments that assert the incommensurable nature of separate linguistic and cultural communities. He argues that if the experiences and beliefs of one community are translatable into the language of another community, then it cannot sensibly be claimed that the two communities constitute wholly self-contained, incommunicable epistemological and linguistic worlds. On the other hand, if they are wholly incommensurate, it would not be possible even to make a claim for being incommensurate. If another world were to be totally unknowable we would not logically be able to know that it was different. If we can even speak of or recognise the difference between two conceptual worlds or schemes then clearly they are to some extent knowable. Davidson says, 'Without a vast common ground there can be no place for disputants to stand in their quarrel' (Davidson 1984: 200).

In his thinking about language, Davidson, in sharp contrast to Derrida, privileges speech over writing and in particular intersubjective speech rather than monologue. Davidson elaborates a triangular dynamic interaction between speaker, respondent and world. He accepts the common postmodern assumption that the world as we know it is always an interpreted world, and that there is no contact with a reality unmediated by language. Yet, he argues, this does not mean there is no such thing as objective knowledge. Language as a practice can only coherently be thought of as **dialogic**, that is, as an interaction between at least two speaking subjects. An entirely private language is simply inconceivable. Further, in order to have the basis for mutual understanding of another's speech there must be a reasonably common view of the world. Finally, it is highly implausible to assume that speakers able to understand or interpret each other could be in massive error as to their shared reality. Davidson argues that 'successful communication proves the existence of a shared, and largely true, view of the world' (Davidson 1984: 201). Even to assume that a person who speaks in an unknown language is speaking rather than emitting random sounds is to accept that he or she shares conceptual beliefs that form the common basic 'grammar' of speech possibility: a notion of truth and meaning, a positional notion of self and other, a notion of difference and sameness, of sequence, of reference and so on. Such features are the foundation of *any* intelligible language and in their absence there could be nothing to sustain either agreement or disagreement.

Yet although speech is thus predicated upon fundamental shared conceptual ground, it is equally, for Davidson, always approximate. There is rarely an exact one-to-one correspondence or translation between the meanings of two speakers. To communicate effectively we must continually adjust our own 'truth-theories' to accommodate the perspective of the other speaker. Davidson argues that all interlocutors start from a 'prior theory' that constitutes their view of the world. In any speech act the participants implicitly assume that there is shared agreement on beliefs and interpretations, that their 'prior theories' are in accord. When speakers encounter disagreement, they adopt a 'passing theory' as a way of adjusting their assumptions to the new perspective so as to maximise agreement. Davidson's term for this is 'interpretive charity' (Davidson 1986: 433–46). The willingness to make sense of another's speech is a pre-condition of communication. From this perspective, speaking is always something of a mutual guessing game. In contrast to Fish's notion of interpretive communities in which the same pool of common meanings can only be endlessly recycled, Davidson's notion of interpretive charity puts creative activity at the heart of language practice. The vision of language that emerges from Davidson's work 'is one of human linguistic behaviour as a highly dynamic, open-ended activity in which we constantly adjust our linguistic usage with the intent of helping our listeners adjust their truth-theories to converge sufficiently to ours to enable communication' (Gorman 1993: 205). This is not naively to rule out discursive and ideological conflict. What Davidson is getting at is that to disagree entails considerable conceptual agreement between disputants. Disagreement in fact becomes the dialectical push towards linguistic and epistemological innovation and learning. Reading a realist novel can be seen as providing excellent training in the practice of 'interpretive charity'. As we begin the first page of a fiction, we start to interpret characters, states of affairs and events on the basis of our 'horizon of expectations' as Jauss calls it, or our 'prior theory' according to Davidson. Subsequent narrative information calls upon us continually to adjust our assumptions, to invent new interpretations so as to accommodate new perspectives.

JÜRGEN HABERMAS AND COMMUNICATIVE REASON

'Interpretive charity' is an apposite term for this co-operative, willing interactive pursuit of meaning. It is also, quite clearly, a rational activity although one that is very different from a subject/object form of knowledge in which the rational individual seeks to 'grasp' (the metaphor is instructive) an aspect of the external world perceived as a passive matter of fact. Interactive reason is close to the ideal of intersubjective or communicative reason put forward by Jürgen Habermas as an alternative to the subject-centred or individualistic reason as mastery of the world that has come to be associated with the Enlightenment. Habermas is reluctant to abandon the universal ideals of democracy, justice, and freedom that he sees as the inheritance of the Enlightenment even if they have been subsequently misshaped by the will to power.

Habermas's concept of communicative reason derives from the view that a major function of language in the everyday world, as in more specialised realms like law, science, and morality, is that of problem solving and validity testing. It is this imperative to deal practically with the world that gives speech its 'illocutionary force'. This is a term Habermas takes from British speech-act theorist, J.L. Austin, to refer to the effective power of speech, most apparent in the making of promises, giving orders, but also in making factual or ethical claims. The marriage contract enacted by saying the words 'I do' is often used as a clear example of illocutionary force, as are commands like 'Attention' or 'Shut the door'. Yet, once thought of performatively within an actual speech situation, even a statement about the world like 'It's hot today' has illocutionary force in that it requires assent or dissent from the other participants in the speech act. For this reason, Habermas places the process of truth and validity testing at the centre of linguistic practice generally. This performative understanding of language is very different from that based upon a correspondence notion of truth in which words and statements are required to match or copy an external existing state of affairs. Habermas comments that the work of Davidson has overcome 'this fixation on the fact-mirroring function of language' (Habermas 1987: 312). Subsequently, Habermas goes on to elaborate a much expanded notion of validity and truth to that of correspondence or verisimilitude, utilizing a performative notion of speech that bears close resemblance to Davidson's triangular relationship of speaker, responder, world.

Rational knowledge as understood from the conventional perspective of a subject/object relation to the world, or, in other words, as an active, knowing individual consciousness that understand the world as a passive object, inevitably tends towards a view of knowledge as mastery. 'By contrast,' Habermas argues, 'as soon as we conceive of knowledge as communicatively mediated, rationality is assessed in terms of the capacity of responsible participants to orient themselves in relation to validity claims geared to intersubjective recognition' (Habermas 1987: 314). Habermas suggests that the system of personal pronouns educates speakers in perspective translation that moves across objective, communal and personal worlds. Once ideas of knowledge and truth are thought of within the intersubjective context of actual speech situations, any notion of verifiability as simply a correspondence between words and world becomes inadequate. In any actual speech situation, utterances are structured upon three components that accord formally to the perspectives of third, second and first person pronouns. There is the impersonal third person perspective for representing states of affairs in the world: 'There are more professional musicians in Liverpool than in any other British city.' In actual speech situations, such propositional statements are always directed towards a second person respondent even if that respondent is the reader of a text book. This relationship can be made explicit by extending the sentence to: 'You may or may not know that there are more professional musicians in Liverpool than in any other British city.' This extended form also makes apparent the illocutionary force of all statements about the world in that they always implicitly require a response either of assent or disagreement from those participating in the speech act. This performative function can be understood as a form of bearing witness. Finally the first person perspective can be brought out by changing the form to 'I believe that there are more professional musicians in Liverpool than in any other British city.' For Habermas these three components, that I have unpacked here, are contained within all performative propositional statements about events and states of affairs. Once this is recognised, notions of truth, validity and knowledge become complicated with normative judgements and values that exceed simple issues of accurate correspondence.

Wolfgang Iser suggests that realist novels produce knowledge of the world by foregrounding the 'repertoires' that structure acts of social communication. An analysis of South African novelist Nadine Gordimer's (1923–) realist novel, *The Conservationist* (1972) offers a fictional demonstration of how the grammar of pronouns might function to orientate consciousness towards different forms of knowledge and truth. The protagonist of the story, Mehring, a successful international investment director, buys land to farm as a form of weekend indulgence he can now afford. Even so, 'he made it his business to pick up a working knowledge of husbandry, animal and crop, so that he couldn't easily be hoodwinked by his people there and could plan farming operations with authority' (Gordimer 1978: 23). This encapsulates the dominant qualities of the character. Mehring has a confident belief in the power of money to meet all his needs. He finds a 'special pleasure in having a woman you've paid for...You've bought and paid for everything' (Gordimer 1978: 77–8). Additionally, as with the farm, he associates knowledge in a wholly functional way with authority and mastery. This is expressed most forcefully in his use of the third person mode when thinking of the African workers on his farm, the neighbouring Indian family of shopkeepers, and even in his thoughts of his son and his mistress. The use of the third person facilitates an easy move from the particular to the general that positions those so known as passive objects within a totalising overview that always exceeds them. For Mehring, the Indian storekeeping neighbours are 'affable as only shop-keeping Jews and Indians are' (Gordimer 1978: 197). Thinking complacently about Jacobus who manages the farm in his absence, he concedes, 'his old boy does better than any white manager. What this really means is that they're more honest than any white you're likely to get in a menial yet responsible position....he hasn't the craft to crook you....you can always trust a man who can't write not to keep a double set of books' (Gordimer 1978: 145). In his relations with his son and mistress, where power is more contested, he resorts to a sense of superior knowledge even more explicitly to secure his authority: 'He knew all the answers she could have given, knew them by heart, had heard them mouthed by her kind a hundred times' (Gordimer 1978: 70–1). His son's resistance to conscription in the South African army is similarly reduced to the typical: 'What is it *he* wants – a special war to be started for him, so that he can prove himself the conscientious objector hero?' (Gordimer 1978: 79). Within the representation of Mehring's consciousness, social relations are wholly understood in terms of subject/object mastery. Other people are objects to be possessed by money and by knowledge: 'He has them up, arraigned, before him [in his thoughts] and they have no answer. Nothing to say. He feels inside himself the relief and overflow of having presented the unanswerable facts. To prevail is to be recharged' (Gordimer 1978: 79–80).

This relationship of mastery is most fully figured in his use of a telephone answering device to which he listens but 'gives no answer. He takes no part in the conversation'. He hears the voices and invitations of his acquaintances in the attitude of 'a doctor or other disinterested confidant, reliably impersonal' (Gordimer 1978: 201). This image conveys a perception of self as in complete control but the irony is that by this stage in the story Mehring's self-sufficiency is unravelling. This is charted linguistically in the text by a shift in pronoun use towards the second and first persons. Even while he defends himself from social contact by using an answering machine he begins to imagine conversations he would have should his son or ex-wife or ex-mistress actually phone him. These imaginary conversations are conducted in a more intersubjective mode than his earlier thought patterns that utilised predominantly third person forms. In his fantasy talk with his mistress he actually uses the communal words 'us' and 'we' to recognise shared experience and perspective: 'That's what you really like about me, about us; we wrestle with each other on each other's ground' (Gordimer 1978: 223). Prior to this, on New Year's Eve, Mehring has become aware of

Jacobus as a person not just as an African worker to be classified and 'known' under that reductive category. This realisation takes the form of an acknowledgement of a lack of knowledge and authority. Wondering whether Jacobus has sons, he thinks 'I ought to know' and he goes on to admit that Jacobus probably knows more about cattle stock than he does (Gordimer 1978: 207). This leads him on to think that they can 'talk together about cattle, there's that much in common'. From there the conversation elaborates dream-like in his head into a sense of shared fellowship denoted by the pronoun 'we': 'But we're getting along fine. We're laughing a lot;' (Gordimer 1978: 208).

It is all a fantasy, though: 'Jacobus has not come' (Gordimer 1978: 209). For most of the story, Mehring clings to a functional form of knowledge that seems to promise mastery. Yet, his objectivising the world by means of impersonal third person mode of discourse, actually keeps him unknowing of the multiplicity and particularity of social reality. He imagines that he and his African workers exist in incommensurate worlds but his ignorance is due to lack of intersubjective communication with them. He never enters into their perspective so as to share their knowledge of their world. Thinking about his son, he wonders 'But were they referring to the same things when they talked together?' (Gordimer 1978: 134). Shared knowledge is produced by movement across the first and second person subject positions and it is a co-operative, ongoing form of understanding that is produced.

Habermas argues that what distinguishes literary language from everyday and scientific and legal discourses is that literary language lacks illocutionary force. It is not involved in the problem solving and validity testing in the same direct way as language that is participating in the world's transactions and business. This neutralising of a speech act's normal binding force empowers it 'for the playful creation of new worlds – or, rather, for the pure demonstration of the world-disclosing force of innovative linguistic expressions' (Habermas 1987: 201). This 'world-disclosing' force of literary language, Habermas claims, binds together the particular with the universal. In order to satisfy readers who are not held by the illocutionary force of dealing with the world's on-going business, a literary text has to be recognised as worth the telling. Habermas claims, 'In its content, a tellable text reaches beyond the local context of the immediate speech situation and is open to further elaboration' (Habermas 1987: 203). Literary language, unlike scientific language, is characterised by its capacity for the creative imagining of other possible worlds.

Yet the division of language function between the discourses of literature and science is perhaps not quite so distinct as Habermas suggests. In an attack upon the prevailing paradigm of anti-realism, philosopher of science, Christopher Norris, points out that the presence of figurative language and metaphor within scientific writing does not invalidate it as a form of rational knowledge. Utilising a notion of translation and following Aristotle's defence of poetic rhetoric, Norris argues that 'metaphors – [especially] those which involve the analogical transfer of attributes from one category or kind of object to another – are able to provide genuine knowledge or even (on occasion) a decisive advance in scientific understanding' (Norris 1997: 105). The most dramatic example of this is some of the language used to translate the mathematical logic of quantum mechanics into verbal logic. The difficulty of expressing this new science in any straightforward empirical discourse has been taken as support for incommensurate worlds. Yet, Norris claims, as the theory of subatomic particles has become more developed and understood, and its explanatory powers across a range of scientific fields recognised, it 'renders implausible any wholesale scepticism with regard to [its] realist credentials' (Norris 1997: 176). From the perspective of the ideal of scientific knowledge as a continuing attempt to understand the world, Einstein's relativity theory 'is not in the least anti-realist, but on the contrary a great stride towards discovering the underlying structure of reality' (Norris 1997: 228). What marks out the knowledge that constitutes quantum mechanics and relativity theory is that it has come into being through an exercise of imaginative reason or thought experiment that runs ahead of any possible empirical observation or experimentation. It is knowledge derived from the fictional invention of possible worlds. Like literary invention and experimentation, scientific pursuit of knowledge is freed from the illocutionary force attached to the everyday business of the world. Within that freedom, thought experiments have a legitimate function in the production of knowledge. Yet in accordance with the defining contract that constitutes scientific discourse as scientific, its fictions are always subject to subsequent validity testing according to mathematical consistency, experimentation and empirical observation.

The possible worlds of realist fiction are not subject to analogous proof of validity but realism is based on a defining commitment to the belief that there is a shared material world external to textuality and subjective, solipsistic worlds. In *Sketches by Boz* the narrator, Boz, turns to implied readers and invites them 'Conceive the situation of a man, spending his last night on earth in this [condemned prisoner's] cell' (Dickens [1836–7] 1995: 246). In Chapter 2, I described that performative gesture as a referential generalisation. All words are substitutions for that which is not present but the recognition of a gesturing towards a non-verbal materiality constitutes the underlying grammar of a consensual realist belief in the possibility of communication about a shared world. Boz's statement simultaneously admits to a specific referential absence, in that the man has to be imagined, and insists that such men do exist in the world. The grammar performs an act of translation between a fictional imagined world and an actual real-world and between the particular and the universal which is a defining feature of realist form. It is this that produces the peculiar illocutionary force of realist writing and that commitment involves novels in the complex communicative reason as set out by Habermas involving judgements incorporating issues of factuality, social rightness, truthfulness and aesthetics.

Such judgements are, of course, less direct and perhaps more complex than many of those dealing with everyday activities tend to be. When reading *Bleak House* we are not looking for a one-to-one correspondence or photographic pictorial match with Victorian society and Victorian London at the mid-century. In order to consider the novel's relationship to its actual referential world we need to be aware of the varied ways in which the text mediates or translates into its fictional world the anxieties, issues and debates of its own time: new state bureaucracy initiated by the Poor Laws of 1834, fears about urban health, the ambitions of a rising professional class, the intense passions aroused by the campaigns over the Corn Laws as the first real challenge to landed interests, the new enthusiasm for photography and so on. This approach to the text, closely aligned to New Historicism, aims to generate a form of knowledge of some of the ideological forces constitutive of mid-nineteenth century social reality. Yet beyond the remit of New Historicism a communicative notion of knowledge would claim that in thus referring to states of affairs in the non-textual world, the novel subjects the reader to the imperative of a normative judgement. In one episode of the story the main protagonists, Esther Summerson and Mr Jarndyce come upon a family of three orphaned children valiantly assuming adult responsibilities in order to survive. Jarndyce says, 'Look at this! For God's sake look at this!' (Dickens [1852–3] 1996: 226). The exclamation makes explicit the normative illocutionary force of bearing witness conjoined to the issue of factuality. If such is the state of affairs, then some evaluative attitude towards it is required of the reader/responder. This in turn brings to the fore the issue of 'truthfulness' or intentionality which we may think about in terms of the author or more productively in terms of the voice or voices of the text. In the case of *Bleak House*, the indignation the text invites the reader to share at the neglect of the individualised children of the poor is dissipated in the passages that represent urban poverty in the mass. Confronted by the horror of city slums the text elicits fear and loathing rather than compassion and outrage. Nevertheless this thematic contradiction between the sympathy generated by the particular as opposed to the fear evoked by mass is formally foregrounded by means of the novel's experimental perspective shifts from third person omniscience to first person narrative. In untangling these tangled threads that constitute the text, the reader is constantly moving across ultimately inseparable issues of form and reference. In this way, Habermas's extended understanding of communicative reason provides a theoretical underpinning for a wide range of critical approaches to literary texts.

To bring together the ideas and debates set out in Part IV and in earlier chapters I shall consider a story that actually has been translated into English from the very different language of Bengali. The fictional world of 'Douloti the Bountiful' by Mahasweta Devi, translated by Gayatri Chakravorty Spivak, is that of the persecuted indigenous tribal people of India. Devi explains, in an authorial conversation that precedes the tales, that India belonged to the tribals long before the incursion of the Aryan-speaking peoples. The tribals have their own quite distinct culture from that of mainstream India and their very different value system, that having no sense of private property, has left them exposed to gross exploitation and marginalisation. Devi says, 'Each tribe is like a continent. But we never tried to know them' (Devi 1995: xxi).

Yet, that absence of knowledge is not due to the incommensurate quality of tribal life, it serves the interests of the mainstream Indian communities only too well. Devi's purpose in her journalism and her fiction is not to preserve some irreducible ethnicity but, on the contrary, to further the 'demand for the recognition of the tribal as a citizen of independent India' (Devi 1995: xvii). Moreover, she moves from the particularity of this cause to the universal plight of 'all the indigenous people of the world'. Nevertheless, Spivak's 'Preface' as translator is somewhat anxious or defensive in tone as to the status of her translation. This is not too surprising given her theoretical affiliation with deconstruction and her earlier essay 'Can the Subaltern Speak?' (Spivak [1988] 1993: 66–111) which suggests the question has to be answered in the negative. She concludes her Preface by quoting the warning contained in the South African writer, J.M. Coetzee's comments on his translation of the Dutch poet Achterberg:

> It is in the nature of the literary work to present its translator with problems for which the perfect solution is impossible...There is never enough closeness of fit between languages for formal features of a work to be mapped across from one language to another without shift of value...Something must be 'lost'.
>
> (Spivak [1988] 1993: xxviii)

While acknowledging the inevitability of loss in the process of all translation, and that includes the translation of experiential reality into representational form, we can also bear in mind Davidson's sense that almost all communication involves a degree of unmapped territory between the conceptual schemes of two speakers. The act of interpretive charity with which we attempt to cross or bridge that gap calls up a creative impulse that carries the potential for innovative thinking and new possible worlds.

The world of Devi's fiction is structured by a chronotopic imagination; that is, she locates her protagonists at the juncture of intermeshing geographical and historical forces. In the story, 'Douloti the Bountiful', Douloti is the daughter of a bonded labourer, a system of conscripted work introduced by the British. While Douloti's knowledge is confined to that of her impoverished village world, her short life is determined by forces that move unhindered across the spatial scales of local, regional, national and international geography. The predominant medium of translation across these different worlds is money. The system of bonded labour was officially abolished by the independent national Indian government in 1976. It has continued to exist on a widespread scale, nevertheless, because the poverty of the tribals enforces them into taking loans at enormous rates of interest from high-caste Indian landowners working in collusion with local government officials and police. The compound interest ensures that the loans can never be repaid and the whole family is bonded to labour for life. Local, national and international industrial contractors collude with traditional landowners to contract tribals as a cheap labour force. Frequently, wives and daughters are taken away to brothels to work for the always outstanding debt. There, they service the sexual market created by the fluidity of modern capitalist development; their customers are largely itinerant regional, national and international contractors, officials and labourers.

In the case of Douloti in the story, the new democratic emancipatory rhetoric of national independence and the traditional religious veneration for the figure of the mother as symbol of Mother India are braided together to translate the brutal economic exploitation that delivers her into sexual slavery. In paying off the loan that keeps Douloti's father in bondage in exchange for 'marriage' to his daughter, the Brahmin procurer boasts that he is prompted solely by religious and nationalist egalitarian principles: 'We are all the offspring of the same mother...Mother India...Hey, you are all independent India's free people' (Devi 1995: 41).

This slick translation between the languages of different value systems or conceptual schemes indicates their commensurability. Indeed, in Devi's stories generally it is the ease of translatability between the residual religious order of things and Western secular materialism that facilitates the transposition of democratic ideology into new mechanisms of oppression. It is the powerless poor who lack the means to operate across different systems: Douloti lacks the knowledge to perceive the interconnections between the larger economic world and her particular suffering. She has literally no alternative but to understand the horror and pain of her life as somehow inevitable and unchangeable: 'The boss has made them land. He plows and plows their bodies' land and raises a crop....Why should Douloti be afraid? She has understood now that this is natural.' (Devi 1995: 60–1). The world of the tribals within Devi's fiction, as without, is one of mass exploitation and victimisation but it is not represented as a world hermetically sealed into a passive fatalism. In 'Douloti the Bountiful', Douloti has an uncle, Bono, who escapes the enclosure of a life already determined by geographical and caste position at birth. He declares, 'I don't hold with work fixed by birth' (Devi 1995: 23). His refusal to accept bondage appears to make no difference to village existence. Yet the story of Bono changes the known reality; it fractures the perceived closure of an enslaved social existence and institutes a new collective knowledge:

> The villagers themselves did not talk about this but cutting wheat in Munibar's fields they would look at each other and think, We could not escape the master's clutches. However, one of us has. Bono has escaped.
>
> The women started up the harvest song whenever they remembered Bono:
>
> Down in the wheat field a yellow bird has come
> O his beak is red.
>
> (Devi 1995: 30)

Bono is subsequently heard of travelling in far market towns, where he 'gets people together with his drum, and tells stories as he sings' (Devi 1995: 35). Bono becomes a political activist. The story imagistically brings together his role as popular artist entertainer, a story-teller and musician, with the potential for revolutionary violence. He describes his killing of an oppressive boss: 'It was as if my two hands did a dance' (Devi 1995: 26).

Bono does not save Douloti. When she is first taken to the brothel at the age of fourteen, the regime there retains enough of traditional respect for hierarchy to allow favoured clients to keep particular women for their own exclusive use. Douloti, as a highly prized virgin, wins such favour with Latia who keeps her for three years. Even though Latia prides himself on bestial displays of virility, this system of patronage protects the favoured prostitutes from further exploitation. However, when a younger generation takes over the running of the brothel the old ways are thrown out for more efficient financial management that has only one ethic: the maximisation of profits. 'The women at Rampiyari's whorehouse were put in a system of twenty to thirty clients by the clock. Pick up your cash fast' (Devi 1995: 79–80). When they become diseased the women are thrown out to beg or die. This is the fate of Douloti. It is Independence Day and children have prepared for the celebrations by drawing the outline of the map of India in the dust, filling it in with coloured liquid chalk. Douloti, trying to crawl back to her village collapses:

> Filling the entire Indian peninsula from the oceans to the Himalayas, here lies bonded labor spread-eagled, kamiya-whore Douloti Nagesia's tormented corpse, putrified with venereal disease, having vomited up all the blood in its dessicated lungs.
>
> (Devi 1995: 93)

Devi's text has a postmodern awareness of the discursive construction of social worlds, especially the powerful mythology within Indian culture of the sacred mother. Her writing highlights the utilisation of religious discourses to enclose women, especially poor tribals, within regulatory mechanism of subservience, obedience and duty. Yet there is an equally uncompromising recognition that discourses are embodied. Devi's realism insists relentlessly on the vulnerable materiality of bodies. In her stories the boundaries of the physical body are broken, dismembered, violated, erupt in disease and putrifaction. This loss of wholeness is mapped onto the ubiquitous flow of money across all borders. The final shocking image of Douloti clearly enacts that translation from the particular to the general that I have associated with realist fiction. However, it is certainly not the kind of shift that Gordimer represents in the consciousness of Mehring in *The Conservationist* whereby he transposes individuals into comfortable, stereotyped generalisation. It is this form of totalising knowledge and universalism that critics of the Enlightenment have condemned as instrumental and collusive with power. The uncompromising realism of Devi's language cuts across the mystifying rhetoric that universalises the nation as one people of

Mother India to insist upon the open, perishable bodies of all of its particular subjects.

Devi's stories eschew any authoritative narrative voice: they are a complex intertextuality of many voices. Single sentences move through different value systems. One ideological world is continually juxtaposed to another. In this sense they are constructed upon the principle of intersubjective communication. As such, they offer a caution against Habermas's rather uncritical advocacy of communicative reason. The exploitative characters in Devi's fiction have no difficulty in occupying the second person position of those they are addressing, but the rationality they bring to bear on this is wholly instrumental. They exploit their respondent's perspective to further their own self-interest. Yet it is of course the formal structure of Devi's prose that foregrounds this. As Wolfgang Iser argues, literary texts represent the linguistic conventions of everyday discourse in such a way that the play of power in intercommunicative relations is thematised (Iser 1980: 74). Devi's texts are constructed entirely as an interweave of social voices. They are, of course, only fictional voices that articulate relations of power and subservience but have no direct bearing on the non-fictional world. What provides the illocutionary force of the stories is their emancipatory project. The implied conceptual or ideological given, that which constitutes the grounds of possibility for meaningful reading, is a passionate commitment to universal ideals of justice and freedom. It is only within that conceptual scheme for evaluating human existence that the exploitation that structures Devi's narratives can find definitional space to stand.

In her Inaugural Andre Deutsch Lecture, given on 22 June 2002, Nadine Gordimer asserted that a writer's 'awesome responsibility' to their craft is that of witness (citations from an edited extract in *The Guardian*, 15 June 2002). She traces this sense of commitment to an incident in her youth when she watched a white intern suturing a black miner's gaping head wound without anaesthetic because 'They don't feel like we do'. She argues that what literary witness writing achieves, in distinction from documentary evidence and photographs, is the imaginative fusion of the duality of the particular with the wider human implications. Yet, any overdue privileging of the formal and writerly is rejected; Gordimer claims it is the pressure of the reality that the writer struggles to bear witness to that imposes the form of the work. She quotes as her witness Albert Camus's declaration, 'The moment when I am no more than a writer I shall cease to be a writer.' Camus is correct in the widest sense, no writer is ever just a writer. Realism as a form is witness to that juncture between the experiential and the representational.

Throughout this chapter, I have drawn upon realist stories recently written in many parts of the world. There seems no better way of substantiating the continued vitality and relevance of the realist genre in a global but highly differentiated geographical and social reality. I have dealt mainly with novelistic prose, largely through constraints of space. However, my definition of realism as performative and based upon a consensual contract with the reader that communication about a non-textual reality is possible can apply equally to poetry and drama and to parts of texts that otherwise foreground textuality or fantasy. It is impossible to prove with mathematical certainty that when we talk or write about a real-world we are not in massive error or wholly enclosed within an ideological order of things. It is, however, equally impossible to prove beyond doubt the incommensurate relativity of separate worlds. What is at stake is the possibility of community and the potential to make new worlds. This is the inherent utopianism of realism as art form.

GLOSSARY

Aesthetic: the Greek derivation of the word refers to things perceptible by the senses. The current usage pertains to the appreciation of the beautiful, or the formal attributes, arrangement and qualities of objects and works of art rather than their utility or meaning.

Anti-humanism *see* **Humanism.**

Art for art's sake/*l'art pour l'art*: a movement initially associated with a group of poets and novelists in mid-nineteenth century France who, somewhat polemically, claimed that the only proper concern of the artist, as artist, is with the formal demands of their art. They thus rejected any social or political role for art. This prioritising of *l'art pour l'art* became an influential aesthetic ideal throughout Europe during the latter part of the nineteenth century and first decades of the twentieth.

Capitalism: in Marxist economic theory 'capital' refers to the fund or stock of money that finances industrial and commercial undertakings. Capitalism is thus the name given to a social and cultural formation or social system that is predominantly organised and structured by the use of private wealth to own and control for profit-making the production and distribution of goods and services.

Classic realist: given nineteenth-century novelists' rejection of classical rules of decorum in art, this is a rather paradoxical label used primarily to refer to nineteenth-century realist fiction. It implies a paradigm or ideal of realism as a coherent body of aesthetic principles that in practice no one novel ever complied with. As a short-hand term it has some use in referring to novels produced while a positive view of human knowledge and communication prevailed.

Closure: as a critical term this refers to the resolution of problems, mystery, uncertainty so as to produce a sense of comprehensively known meaning to a text, to a character, a theme, and to words. *See also* **Totalising.**

Conceptual scheme: an intellectual or abstract system of understanding that has a self-contained unity of meaning or intelligibility.

Dialogic: the term derives from the work of Russian linguist and critic, Mikhail Bakhtin. Bakhtin uses it to suggest that words *in use* have to be understood as always engaged in 'dialogue' with other words: words in practice, whether written, spoken or only thought, are necessarily embedded in social contexts. This social existence of words entails that they are always freighted with echoes and intonations of their meanings in previous usage, while at the same time any speaker's present intentional meaning will be influenced by the expected response their words will elicit.

***Différance*:** a term coined by Jacques Derrida to bring together the notions of deferral and difference as constitutive of language. The word *'différance'* demonstrates graphically Derrida's claim that writing is not a supplement of speech in that only the written form can make the difference and oscillation or deferral of denoted meaning apparent. For a French speaker there is no distinction in sound between *différence* and *différance*.

Discursive network: a discourse is usually taken to denote a socially and historically situated use of language, which is sustained and demarcated by shared vocabulary, assumptions, values and interests, as for example a medical or legal discourse. A discursive network thus denotes an interconnected system of different discourses that nevertheless share or produce a common area of perceived knowledge. For example, we might understand the cultural perception of 'delinquency' as produced by a discursive network that would include journalistic discourse, academic sociological discourse, political discourse, moral and religious discourse, and novelistic discourse.

Empiricism: an approach to knowledge that rejects metaphysics, purely abstract thinking, and idealism. Empirical knowledge is that acquired through sensory observation and experimentation. British empiricism is associated with the philosophical tradition that includes Francis Bacon (1561–1626), Thomas Hobbes (1588–1679), John Locke (1632–1704) and David Hume (1711–76).

Enlightenment: sometimes called Age of Reason, it is the era of the eighteenth century characterised by the intellectual espousal of progressive ideals of liberty, justice and democracy and an emphasis on rational, moral and scientific improvement of human existence. Religious mystery and all forms of superstitious belief were displaced in favour of empiricist, naturalist and materialist understanding of the world.

Episteme: a term associated with the work of Michel Foucault and used to refer to a fundamental underlying structure or set of rules that produces the entire lived and known reality, the discourses and practices of any particular epistemic era of history. In that sense an episteme constitutes a cultural totality. *See also* **Conceptual scheme, Totalising.**

Epistemology: the branch of philosophy that deals with the nature, source, reliability and scope of knowledge.

Fascism: the principles, system of thought, and organisation of authoritarian, nationalistic movements. Fascism was first instituted as a political movement in Italy in the early part of the twentieth century whence it spread to Germany. The term is currently used more loosely to denote any extreme right-wing authoritarianism.

Focalisation: a critical term used by Gérard Genette to denote the aspect of narrative that orders the perspective from which events and characters are perceived by the reader. At times a story may be focalised through the viewpoint of one particular character while at other times the narrator controls the viewpoint. What is important to grasp is that focalising can be quite separate from the voice that narrates.

Formalism: as a critical term, formalism refers to an approach to verbal and visual art that concentrates upon the form, structures and techniques of the work rather than its subject matter, meaning or historical context.

Free indirect discourse/speech: a literary critical term that refers to passages of narration in which aspects of a character's language, in terms of vocabulary, tone of voice, values and perspectives, invade the third person narrative discourse but are not separated out or distinguished by means of inverted commas as in direct character speech. Bakhtin refers to this kind of writing as 'double-voiced discourse' in that two different social voices, usually a character's and a narrator's, co-exist in the same passage.

Functionalism: an understanding, interpretation or valuation of things in terms of the functions they fulfil.

Grand narratives: a term used by Jean-François Lyotard to refer to cultural narratives such as those that order and legitimise scientific notions of knowledge and political ideals of justice, progress and liberty. Lyotard argues that two grand narratives predominate: an Enlightenment narrative of human emancipation from the bondage of ignorance and oppression and a more philosophical narrative concerned with the evolution of a self-conscious human subjectivity or spirit. By terming them 'narratives' Lyotard points up their cultural fabrication.

Humanism: a term used initially to characterise the intellectual culture of Renaissance Europe. Contrary to the God-centred, fatalistic medieval view of existence, Renaissance scholars and artists responded optimistically to human achievement in arts and sciences and celebrated the human potential to ever increase rational knowledge of the world and human nature. In general terms 'humanism' refers to a secular understanding of humanity that emphasises people's rational understanding, agency, and progressive capacities. **Anti-humanism** rejects this human-centred optimism and perceives human beings as lacking autonomy, self-knowledge and objective understanding of the world. Current versions of anti-humanism stem from structuralist and poststructuralist perceptions that 'reality' as we experience it is wholly determined without any human individual intervention by the pre-existing impersonal orders of language and culture.

Illocutionary acts: a term used by speech-act philosopher and theorist J. Austin (1911–1960) to refer to the performative aspect of speech or utterances, for example a warning, a promise, or an order. In contrast to a philosophical concern with how words mean, Austen directs attention to their 'illocutionary force', the effect they produce in the world.

Implied reader: the kind of reader that the text itself seems to assume in the language register deployed, in the values that are taken for granted, in direct addresses to such a reader and in the handling of perspective and point of view. In the strong sense of this, texts can be thought of as calling the reader into being: in the act of complying with the textual attributes listed above we unconsciously align ourselves with the kind of reader the text requires or implies.

Incommensurate worlds: material and/or mental realities that share no common measure or standard of likeness in any degree or part.

Langue: a term used by Swiss linguist Ferdinand de Saussure (1857–1913) to refer to language as an overall system of meaning, as it exists at any single moment of time, or synchronically. '*Langue*' in this sense approximates to the rather abstract notion of 'human language' or a total perception of a national language like English. Contrasting to this, is language as it occurs throughout history – diachronically – in actual utterances that people speak or write. The multiple and infinitely diverse utterances, speech in actuality, Saussure terms **parole**. His scientific project, never fulfilled, was to understand how the finite system of '*langue*' could produce the endless proliferation of *parole*.

Literary field: French sociologist, Pierre Bourdieu, uses this term to designate the cultural space in which writers write. It is a space structured by earlier traditions of different genres, by the cultural values attached to different forms of writing, by the amount of prestige awarded to the new or the established forms, and so on. All writers have perforce to position themselves within this cultural space in terms of choices of what style, form and genre they adopt.

Marxism: the political and economic theories of Karl Marx (1818–83) and their subsequent development by later Marxist thinkers. Marx was opposed to all forms of idealism, expounding a materialist understanding of history and culture as determined by the prevailing mode of production at any historical time. His economic theories are grounded upon the ultimate contradiction of capitalism to labour.

Mimesis: a critical term deriving from Greek drama to refer to the dramatic imitation of words and actions by actors. In current usage it refers to the representation of the real world in visual and verbal art.

Modernism: a European phase of innovative and experimental art and thought occuring at the end of the nineteenth century and approximately the first three decades of the twentieth century. It was largely characterised by a rejection of the artistic, social and moral conventions and values of a previous generation.

Narratology: the study of the rules of combination and sequence, the structures and the formal conventions that produce narratives of all kinds.

Narrator: the voice that tells the story in either the first or third person.

An **omniscient narrator** is one that has knowledge of all events in the story and access to the thoughts and feelings of all characters.

Naturalism: an artistic approach and literary and artistic movement usually associated with the declared aims of Emile Zola (1840–1902) and the critical and historical writing of French scholar Hyppolite Taine (1828–93). The central emphasis is on the force of biological determinism and heredity upon human life and society. Their critics often accuse naturalist writers and artists of undue concern with the most degrading and bestial aspects of existence.

Negative critique: a cultural and artistic analysis that places value upon the ability of a literary work to reveal oppressive and authoritarian elements in the existing social formation or in the prevailing perception of what constitutes social reality.

New Historicism: a historicised approach to writing strongly influenced by the work of Michel Foucault. Typically, New Historicists do not privilege literary texts above other textual forms; literary texts are read as participating in discursive networks that sustain and expand structures of power. *See also* **discursive network**.

Objective *see* **Relative truth.**

Paradigm: a mode of viewing the world or a model of reality which underlies scientific and philosophical theories at a particular moment of history. *See also* **conceptual scheme**.

Parole *see* **Langue**

Particular: pertaining to a single definite thing, person or set of things as opposed to any other. Particular things are the opposite of universals which denote classes or groups of things in general. For example, Stalin as an actual historical person was a particular instance of a universal class we designate 'tyrants' or 'dictators'.

Positivism: a philosophical system elaborated by Auguste Comte (1798–1857) rejecting all metaphysical systems of belief and accepting as human knowledge only positive facts established by means of empirical observation. As a general scientific and philosophical outlook in the nineteenth century positivism was characterised by an optimistic confidence in an empirical approach to the world. *See also* **Empiricism**.

Postmodernism: a term first emerging in American cultural analysis in the 1970s to suggest a new historical social formation to that which had characterised the modernity of cultural and social reality from the Renaissance onwards. The postmodern world is theorised as transnational, empty of any essential or stabilised meaning, and constituted by global markets and consumerism. Within postmodernism the humanist confidence in progress and agency and a realist belief in the communicability of experience gives way to the pessimism of anti-humanism and anti-realism. *See also* **Humanism**.

Readerly: a translation of Roland Barthes' term '*lisible*' which translates literally as legible. Barthes maintains that readerly texts offer themselves to be passively consumed by their readers in so far as they challenge no conventional assumptions either in their use of artistic form or in their handling of subject matter. *See also* **Writerly**.

Relative truth: a notion of veracity that makes no absolute claims to being universally true for all cases and all time but holds that truth will vary according to culture and even from individual to individual. **Objective truth** by contrast claims to assert what is in fact the case independent of any relative, cultural or personal circumstances. **Subjective truth** is that which is believed to be and experienced as true by the individual claimant; in the strong sense of limiting truth entirely to individual subjectivity this is referred to as 'solipsism'.

Romance: a narrative form, developed initially in the Romance languages during the twelfth and thirteenth centuries and in English from the fourteenth century. Romance narratives are peopled by nobly born heroes and heroines as well as by magicians and mythical creatures. Adventures take place in unreal landscapes and plots are structured by the marvellous and mystical and celebrate chivalrous ideals.

Romanticism: a European artistic movement occurring roughly between 1770 and 1850, characterised by a strong reaction against Enlightenment rationalism and hence concerned with the 'truths' of the individual imagination, intuition, sensibility and affections.

Self-reflexive: this term brings together the notion of a mirror reflection with the intellectual notion of reflecting as thinking to suggest the capacity to critically overview the self, whether that self be an individual, or a culture, or a creative practice.

Sign: any visual or aural entity that stands for something else and is interpreted in this way by an individual or social group: a red flag is a sign for danger in many western societies, an individual may have their own good luck sign, and words of a language constitute one of the most complex sign systems.

Socialist realism: the form of realism officially adopted at the Congress of Soviet Writers in 1934 as approved by Stalin. This doctrine decreed that art should be realistic and optimistic, showing the proletariat as heroic and idealistic in plot structures that led to positive outcomes. Experimental art was denigrated as decadent and bourgeois.

Subjective   *see* **Relative truth**.

Textuality: as used in current theoretical discourse, this term brings together the original notion of 'text' as the actual words of a written or spoken utterance with the notion of 'texture' to focus upon the materiality of words. This emphasis displaces 'meaning' as an original idea in the mind of the author to the endless process of producing meaning performed by the interweaving of the words themselves.

Totalising: this term is used in current theoretical discourse to suggest an imposed conceptual unity and completeness which ignores or disallows actual existing diversity and non-conclusiveness. *see also* **Closure**, **Conceptual scheme**.

Verisimilitude: having the appearance of being real, a likeness or resemblance to reality. Compared to **mimesis**, verisimilitude implies a weaker notion of exactitude or correspondence and in that way can encompass a wider range of effects within an art work as convincingly life-like or plausible, for example, the singing of a love-song at a tender moment in a film.

Writerly: a translation of Barthes' term *scriptible*; a text which the reader must work to produce or 'write'. Such a text resists 'closure', or confinement to a unitary meaning. *See* **Textuality**.

SUGGESTIONS FOR FURTHER READING

While all the texts cited in this book and listed in the Bibliography are of relevance to those studying realism, the following provide useful starting points to some of the main aspects dealt with in the various chapters.

Founding criticism of literary realism

Aesthetic and Politics: Debates between Bloch, Lukáks, Brecht, Benjamin, Adorno (1980), translation editor Ronald Taylor, London, Verso. [This contains the main essays and responses that articulated the controversy over realism versus experimentalism.]

Auerbach, Erich [1946] (1953) *Mimesis: The Representation of Reality in Western Literature*, translated by Willard T. Trask; Princeton, Princeton University Press. [A brilliant book, this is essential reading for any serious study of realism.]

Lucáks, Georg [1937] (1969) *The Historical Novel*, translated by Hannah and Stanley Mitchell; Harmondsworth, Penguin. [Both of Lukács' works listed here are still the best historicised account of literary realism and indispensable reading.]

—— [1948] (1972), *Studies in European Realism: A Sociological Survey of the Writings of Balzac, Stendhal, Zola, Gorky and Others*, translated by Edith Bone; London, Merlin Press.

Levin, Harry (1963), *The Gates of Horn: A Study of Five French Realists*, New York and Oxford, Oxford University Press. [The first chapters provide an excellent general discussion of the development of nineteenth-century realism.]

Stern, J. P. (1973), *On Realism*, London, Routledge and Kegan Paul. [At times this is a difficult book but full of brilliant insights.]

More recent defences of realist writing

Levine, George (1981) *The Realist Imagination: English Fiction from 'Frankenstein' to 'Lady Chatterley'*, Chicago, Chicago University Press. [The book argues that nineteenth-century writers, far from claiming to offer readers a one-to-one correspondence, were fully aware of the contested nature of reality.]

Shaw, Harry E. (1999) *Narrating Reality: Austen, Scott, Eliot*, Ithaca, New York, Cornell University Press. [This argues for the need to move beyond the current poststructural 'aesthetics of suspicion' and invokes Habermas in the project of re-asserting the credentials of realist writing.]

Reader response approaches to literary realism

Furst, Lilian R. (1995) *All is True: The Claims and Strategies of Realist Fiction*, Durham, Duke University Press.

Rifaterre, Michael (1990) *Fictional Truth*, Baltimore and London, Johns Hopkins University Press.

Formalist approaches to narrative

Gennette, Gerard (1980) *Narrative Discourse: An Essay in Method*, translated by Jane Lewin; Ithaca, New York, Cornell University Press. [A detailed analysis of narrative form based upon extended analyses of Marcel Proust's novel, *A la Recherche du Temps Perdu* (1913–27).]

Rimmon-Kenan, Shlomith (1983) *Narrative Fiction: Contemporary Poetics*, London and New York, Methuen. [A succinct and comprehensive account of formal and structuralist approaches to narrative.]

Realism in the visual arts

Nochlin, Linda (1971) *Realism*, Harmondsworth, Penguin. [Provides a very readable and incisive account of realism in visual art.]

Roberts, John (1998) *The Art of Interruption: Realism, Photography and the Everyday*, Manchester, Manchester University Press. [A rather difficult but stimulating book.]

Anthologies and collections of essays on literary realism

Becker, George (ed.) (1963) *Documents of Modern Literary Realism*, Princeton, Princeton University Press. [Very comprehensive coverage, including American and European sources.]

Furst, Lilian R. (ed.) (1992) *Realism*, London and New York, Longman. [Contains structuralist and postmodern views as well as commentary by Balzac, Dickens, George Eliot and Lukács.]

Hemmings, F. W. J. (ed.) (1974) *The Age of Realism*, Harmondsworth, Penguin. [A collection of essays on realism as practised in many countries, with a useful historical introduction.]

BIBLIOGRAPHY

Adorno, Theodor W. [1967] (1983) *Prisms*, translated by Samuel and Shierry Weber, Cambridge, Massachusetts, Massachusetts Institute of Technology.

Adorno, Theodor W. and Horkheimer, Max [1944] (1997) *Dialectic of Enlightenment*, translated by John Cumming, London, Verso.

Aristotle [350BC] (1963) *Poetics*, translated by John Warrington, London, Dent.

Armstrong, Nancy (1999) *Fiction in the Age of Photography: The Legacy of British Realism*, Cambridge, Massachusetts, Harvard University Press.

Ashcroft, Bill *et al.* (1989) *The Empire Writes Back: Theory and Practice in Postcolonial Literature*, London, Routledge.

Auerbach, Erich [1946] (1953) *Mimesis: The Representation of Reality in Western Literature*, translated by Willard R. Trask, Princeton, Princeton University Press.

Austen, Jane [1818] (1990) *Persuasion*, Oxford, Oxford University Press.

Azim, Firdous (1993) *The Colonial Rise of the Novel*, London, Routledge.

Bakhtin, Mikhail (1981) *The Dialogic Imagination: Four Essays*, translated by Caryl Emerson and Michael Holquist, Austin, University of Texas Press.

Balzac, Honoré de, [1842] (1981) 'The Human Comedy' translated by Petra Morrison in Arnold Kettle (ed.) *The Nineteenth-Century Novel: Critical Essays and Documents*, London, Heinemann.

—— [1846] (1965) *Cousin Bette*, translated by Marion Ayton Crawford, Harmondsworth, Penguin.

Barthes, Roland [1953] (1967) *Writing Degree Zero, and Elements of Semiology*, translated by Annette Lavers and Colin Smith, London, Jonathan Cape

—— (1960) 'The Reality Effect' in Tzvetan Todorov, *French Literary Theory*, translated by R. Carter, Cambridge, Cambridge University Press.

—— [1973] (1990) *S/Z*, translated by Richard Miller, Oxford, Blackwell.

—— (1977) 'Introduction to the Structural Analysis of Narratives' in *Image Music Text*, translated by Stephen Heath, London, Fontana.

Becker, George J. (ed.) (1963) *Documents of Modern Literary Realism*, Princeton, Princeton University Press.

Beer, Gillian (1983) *Darwin's Plots: Evolutionary Narrative in Darwin, George Eliot and Nineteenth-Century Fiction*, London, Routledge and Kegan Paul.

Benjamin, Walter [1955] (1999) 'The Work of Art in the Age of Mechanical Reproduction' in *Illuminations*, translated by Harry Zohn, London, Pimlico.

—— [1955–71] (1983) *Charles Baudelaire: A Lyric Poet in the Era of High Capitalism*, translated by Harry Zohn, London, Verso.

Bourdieu, Pierre (1996) *The Rules of Art: Genesis and Structure of the Literary Field*, translated by Susan Emanuel, Cambridge, Polity Press.

Brecht, Berthold (1977) 'Brecht against Lukács' translated by Ronald Taylor in Ronald Taylor (ed.) *Aesthetics and Politics*, London, Verso.

Brontë, Charlotte [1853] (2000) *Villette*, Oxford, Oxford University Press.

Brooker, Peter (ed.) (1992) *Modernism/Postmodernism*, Harlow, Essex, Longman.

Budgen, Frank (1989) *James Joyce and the Making of 'Ulysses', and other writing*, Oxford, Oxford University Press

Carter, Angela (1984) *Nights at the Circus*, London, Picador.

Chapman, Seymour (1978) *Story and Discourse*, Ithaca, New York, Cornell University Press.

Cohn, Dorrit (1978) *Transparent Minds: Narrative Modes Presenting Consciousness in Fiction*, Princeton, New Jersey, Princeton University Press.

Conrad, Joseph [1897] (1988) *The Nigger of the 'Narcissus'*, Harmondsworth, Penguin.

Culler, Jonathan (1975) *Structuralist Poetics: Structuralist Linguistics and the Study of Literature*, London, Routledge and Kegan Paul.

Currie, Mark (1998) *Postmodern Narrative Theory*, Houndsmills, Basingstoke, Macmillan.

Dasenbrock, Reed Way (1993) (ed.) *Literary Theory after Davidson*, Pennsylvania, Pennsylvania State University Press.

Davidson, Donald (1984) *Inquiries into Truth and Interpretation*, Oxford, Clarendon.

Davidson, Donald (1986) 'A Nice Derangement of Epitaphs' in Ernest LePore (ed.) *Truth and Interpretation: Perspectives on the Philosophy of Donald Davidson*, Oxford, Blackwell.

Davies, Tony (1997) *Humanism*, London, Routledge.

Day, Aidan (1996) *Romanticism*, London, Routledge.

Derrida, Jaques [1967] (1976) *Of Grammatology*, translated by Gayatri Chakravorty Spivak, Baltimore, Johns Hopkins University Press.

Derrida, Jaques [1967] (1978) *Writing and Difference*, translated by Alan Bass, London, Routledge.

Devi, Mahasweta (1995) *Imaginary Maps: Three Stories*, translated by Gayatri Chakravorty Spivak, London, Routledge.

Dickens, Charles [1837–8] (1982) *Oliver Twist*, Oxford, Oxford University Press.

―― [1836–7] (1995) *Sketches by Boz*, Harmondsworth, Penguin.

―― [1852–3] (1996) *Bleak House*, Oxford, Oxford University Press.

―― [1854] (1989) *Hard Times*, Oxford, Oxford University Press.

―― [1860–1] (1965) *Great Expectations*, Harmondsworth, Penguin.

Dimond, Frances and Taylor, Roger (eds) (1987), *Crown and Camera: The Royal Family and Photography*, Harmondsworth, Penguin.

Ejxenbaum, Boris [1927] (1971) 'The Theory of the Formal Method' reprinted in Ladislav Matejka and Krystna Pomorska (eds) *Readings in Russian Poetics: Formalist and Structuralist Views*, Cambridge, Massachusetts, Massachusetts Institute of Technology.

Eliot, George [1859] (1980) *Adam Bede*, Harmondsworrth, Penguin.

—— [1871–2] (1994) *Middlemarch*, Harmondsworth, Penguin.

—— [1874–6] (1988) *Daniel Deronda*, Oxford, Oxford University Press.

Evans, Henry Sutherland (1853) 'Balzac and his Writings: Translations of French Novels', *Westminster Review*, 4 new series, 202.

Fish, Stanley (1981) 'Why no one's afraid of Wolfgang Iser', *Diacritics*, 11 , 7.

Flaubert, Gustave [1857] (1950) *Madame Bovary*, translated by Alan Russell, Harmondsworth, Penguin.

—— [1857] (1961) *Three Tales*, translated by Robert Baldick, Harmondsworth, Penguin.

Forster, John (1892) *The Life of Charles Dickens*, London, Chapman and Hall.

Foucault, Michel [1961] (1965) *Madness and Civilisation*, translated by Richard Howard, London, Random House.

—— [1963] (1979) *Discipline and Punish: The Birth of the Clinic*, translated by Alan Sheridan, Harmondsworth, Penguin.

—— [1969] (1973) *The Archaeology of Knowledge*, translated by Alan Sheridan, London, Tavistock Publications.

—— [1976] (1981) *The History of Sexuality: An Introduction*, translated by Robert Hurley, Harmondsworth, Penguin.

Fraser's Magazine (unattributed essay) (1851) 'W.M. Thackeray and Arthur Pendennis, Esquires', *Fraser's Magazine*, (43) 86.

Gallagher, Catherine (1985) *The Industrial Reformation of English Fiction: Social Discourse and Narrative Form 1832–1867*, Chicago, Chicago University Press.

Gennette, Gerard [1972] (1980) *Narrative Discourse: An Essay in Method*, translated by Jane E. Lewin, Ithaca, New York, Cornell University Press.

Gilbert, Sandra M. and Gubar, Susan (1979) *The Madwoman in the Attic: The Woman Writer and the Nineteenth-Century Literary Imagination*, New Haven, Yale University Press.

Gissing, George (1898) *Charles Dickens: A Critical Study*, London, Blackie and Son.

Gordimer, Nadine (1978) *The Conservationist*, Harmondsworth, Penguin.

Gorman, David (1993) 'Davidson and Dunnett on Language and Interpretation', in Reed Way Dasenbrock (ed.) *Literary Theory after Davidson*, Pennsylvania, Pennsylvania State University Press.

Graham, Kenneth (1965) *English Criticism of the Novel 1865–1900*, Oxford, Clarendon Press.

Greimas, A. J. (1971) 'Narrative Grammar: Units and Levels', *Modern Language Notes*, 86, 793–806.

Habermas, Jürgen (1987) *The Philosophical Discourse of Modernity: Twelve Lectures*, translated by Frederick Lawrence, Oxford, Polity Press.

Hardy, Thomas [1891] (1988) *Tess of the D'Urbervilles*, Oxford, Oxford University Press.

Harvey, David (1990) *The Condition of Postmodernity: An Enquiry into the Origins of Cultural Change*, Oxford, Blackwell.

—— (1996) *Justice, Nature and the Geography of Difference*, Oxford, Blackwell.

—— (2000) *Spaces of Hope*, Edinburgh, Edinburgh University Press.

Hemmings, Frederick W. J. (1953) *Emile Zola*, Oxford, Oxford University Press

Hobsbawn, Eric J. (1975a) *The Age of Revolution 1789–1848*, London, Weidenfeld and Nicolson.

—— (1975b) *The Age of Capital 1848–1875*, London, Weidenfeld and Nicolson.

Holub, Robert C. (1984) *Reception Theory: A Critical Introduction*, London: Methuen.

Homans, Margaret (1995) 'Victoria's Sovereign Obedience: Portraits of the Queen as Wife and Mother' in Carol T. Christ and John O. Jordan (eds) *Victorian Literature and the Victorian Pictorial Imagination*, Berkeley, University of California Press.

Iser, Wolfgang [1976] (1980) *The Act of Reading: A Theory of Aesthetic Response*, Baltimore, Johns Hopkins University Press.

Jakobson, Roman [1921] (1971) 'On Realism in Art' in Ladislav Matejka and Krystna Pomorska (eds) *Readings in Russian Poetics: Formalist and Structuralist Views*, Cambridge, Massachusetts, Massachusetts Institute of Technology.

—— [1956] (1988) 'Two Aspects of Language and Two Types of Aphasic Disturbances' in David Lodge (ed.) *Modern Criticism and Theory: A Reader*, London, Longman.

—— (1960) 'Closing Statement: Linguistics and Poetics' in Thomas A. Sebeok (ed.) *Style in Language*, Cambridge, Massachusetts, Massachusetts Institute of Technology.

Jakobson, R. and Halle, M. (1956) *Fundamentals of Language*, The Hague, Mouton.

Jameson, Fredric (1998) *The Cultural Turn: Selected Writings on the Postmodern 1983–1998*, London, Verso.

James, Henry [1894] (1987) 'The Art of Fiction' in Roger Gard (ed.) *The Critical Muse: Selected Literary Criticism*, Harmondsworth, Penguin.

James, Henry (1914) *Notes on Novelists and Some Other Notes*, London, Dent.

Jauss, Hans Robert (1982) *Toward an Aesthetic of Reception*, translated by Timothy Bahti, Minneapolis, University of Minnesota Press.

Keating, Peter (1989) *The Haunted Study*, London, Fontana Press.

Kuhn, Thomas (1970) *The Structure of Scientific Revolutions*, 2nd edn, Chicago, University of Chicago Press.

Leavis, Frank R. (1972) *The Great Tradition*, Harmondsworth, Penguin.

Levin, Harry (1963) *The Gates of Horn; A Study of Five French Realists*, New York and Oxford, Oxford University Press.

Levine, George (1981) *The English Realist Imagination: English Fiction from Frankenstein to Lady Chatterly*, Chicago, University of Chicago Press.

Lewes, G.H. (1858) 'Realism in Art: Recent German Fiction', *Westminster Review*, 14 new series, 494.

Lodge, David (1972) (ed.) *Twentieth Century Literary Criticism: A Reader*, London, Longman

—— (1977) *Modes of Modern Writing: Metaphor, Metonymy and the Typology of Modern Literature*, London, Edward Arnold.

—— (1988) *Modern Criticism and Theory: A Reader*, London, Longman.

Lukács, Georg [1914–15] (1978) *The Theory of the Novel: A Historico-Philosophical Essay on the Form of Great Epic Literature*, translated by Anna Bostock, London, Merlin Press.

—— [1937] (1969) *The Historical Novel*, translated by Hannah and Stanley Mitchell, Harmondsworth, Penguin.

—— [1948] (1972) *Studies in European Realism: A Sociological Survey of the Writings of Balzac, Stendhal, Zola, Gorky and Others*, translated by Edith Bone, London, Merlin Press.

Lyotard, Jean-François [1979] (1984) *The Postmodern Condition: A Report on Knowledge*, translated by Geoff Bennington and Brian Massumi, Manchester, Manchester University Press.

MacLaverty, Bernard (1998) *Grace Notes*, London, Vintage.

Man, Paul de, (1983) *Blindness and Insight: Essays in the Rhetoric of Contemporary Criticism*, 2nd revised edn, London, Methuen.

Marx, Karl [1852] (1954) *The Eighteenth Brumaire of Louis Bonaparte*, London, Lawrence and Wishart.

Miller, D. A. (1988) *The Novel and the Police*, Berkeley and Los Angeles, University of California Press.

Miller, J Hillis (1971) 'The Fiction of Realism: *Sketches by Boz, Oliver Twist*, and Cruikshank's Illustrations' in Ada Nisbet and Blake Nevius (eds) *Dickens Centennial Essays*, Berkely, University of California Press.

Moi, Toril (1985) *Sexual Textual Politics: Feminist Literary Theory*, London, Methuen.

Norris, Christopher (1997) *New Idols of the Cave: On the Limits of Anti-Realism*, Manchester, Manchester University Press.

Pinney, Thomas (ed.) (1963) *Essays of George Eliot*, London, Kegan Paul.

Plotz, John (2000) *The Crowd: British Literature and Public Politics*, Berkeley and Los Angeles, University of California Press.

Poovey, Mary (1995) *Making a Social Body: British Cultural Formation 1830–1864*, Chicago, University of Chicago Press.

—— (1989) *Uneven Developments: The Ideological Work of Gender in Mid-Victorian England*, London, Virago.

—— (1984) *The Proper Lady and the Woman Writer: Ideology as Style in the Works of Mary Wollstonecraft, Mary Shelley and Jane Austen*, Chicago, Chicago University Press.

Propp, Vladimir [1929] (1971) 'Fairy Tale Transformations', in Ladislav Matejka and Krystna Pomorska (eds) *Readings in Russian Poetics: Formalist and Structuralist Views*, Cambridge, Massachusetts, Massachusetts Institute of Technology.

—— (1968) *Morphology of the Folktale*, translated by L. A. Wagner, Austin, Texas, University of Texas Press.

Proulx, Annie (1993) *The Shipping News*, London, Fourth Estate.

Putnam, Hilary (1990) *Realism with a Human Face* (ed.) James Conant, Cambridge, Massachusetts, Harvard University Press.

Rimmon-Kenan, Shlomith (1983) *Narrative Fiction: Contemporary Poetics*, London, Methuen.

Robey, David (1986) 'Anglo-American New Criticism' in A. Jefferson and D. Robey (eds) *Modern Literary Theory*, 2nd edn, London, Batsford.

Rorty, Richard (1991) *Objectivity, Relativism and Truth: Philosophical Papers*, vol. 1, and *Essays on Heidegger and Others: Philosophical Papers*, vol. 2, Cambridge, Cambridge University Press.

Said, Edward (1984) *The World, the Text and the Critic*, London, Faber and Faber.

—— (1994) *Culture and Imperialism*, London, Vintage.

Saussure, Ferdinand de [1916] (1983) *Course in General Linguistics*, translated by Roy Harris, London, Duckworth.

Selden, Raman (1985) *A Reader's Guide to Contemporary Literary Theory*, Brighton, Harvester.

Shklovsky, Victor [1917] (1988) 'Art as Technique' reprinted in David Lodge (ed.) *Modern Criticism and Theory: A Reader*, London, Longman.

Showalter, Elaine (1978) *A Literature of Their Own*, London, Virago.

Spark, Muriel (1965) *The Prime of Miss Jean Brodie*, Harmondsworth, Penguin.

Spencer, Jane (1986) *The Rise of the Woman Novelist: From Aphra Behn to Jane Austen*, Oxford, Blackwell.

Spivak, Gayari Chakravorty [1988] (1993) 'Can the Subaltern Speak?' in Patrick Williams and Laura Chrisman (eds) *Colonial Discourse and Post-Colonial Theory: A Reader*, Hemel Hempstead, Harvester Wheatsheaf.

—— (1988) *In Other Worlds: Essays in Cultural Politics*, London, Routledge.

Stang, Richard (1959) *The Theory of the Novel in England 1850–1870*, London, Routedge and Kegan Paul.

Stendhal, Frederic de [1839] (1958) *The Charterhouse of Parma*, translated by Margaret R. B. Shaw, Harmondsworth, Penguin.

Stevenson, R. L. (1999) 'A Note on Realism' and 'A Humble Remonstrance' in Glenda Norquay (ed.) *R. L. Stevenson on Fiction: An Anthology of Literary and Critical Essays*, Edinburgh, Edinburgh University Press.

Stone, Donald (1980) *The Romantic Impulse in Victorian Fiction*, Cambridge, Massachusetts, Harvard University Press.

Strachey, Ray [1928] (1978) *The Cause: A Short History of the Women's Movement in Great Britain*, London, Virago.

Taylor, Ronald (ed. and trans.) (1980) *Aesthetics and Politics: Debates Between Bloch, Lukács, Brecht, Bejamin, Adorno*, London, Verso.

Thackeray, W. M. [1850] (1996) *The Newcomes, Memoirs of a Most Respectable Family*, Ann Arbour, University of Michegan Press.

—— [1850] (1994) *Pendennis*, Oxford, Oxford University Press.

Tombs, Robert (1996) *France 1814–1914*, London, Longman.

Watt, Ian [1957] (1987) *The Rise of the Novel: Studies in Defoe, Richardson and Fielding*, London, Hogarth Press.

Williams, Raymond (1965) *The Long Revolution*, Harmondsworth, Penguin.

—— (1974) *The English Novel from Dickens to Lawrence*, Frogmore, St Albans, Paladin.

Wittgenstein, Ludwig [1933–35] (1972) *The Blue and Brown Books: Preliminary Studies in 'Philosophical Investigations'*, Oxford, Blackwell.

—— [1945–49] (1972) *Philosophical Investigations*, translated by G. E. M. Anscombe, Oxford, Blackwell.

Woolf, Virginia [1924] (1967) 'Mr Bennett and Mrs Brown' in *Collected Essays*, vol. 1, London, Hogarth Press.

—— [1925] (1972) 'Modern Fiction' in *Collected Essays*, vol. 2, London, Hogarth Press

—— [1925] (1992) *Mrs Dalloway*, Harmondsworth, Penguin.

Zola, Emile [1885] (1954) *Germinal*, translated by Leonard Tancock, Harmondsworth, Penguin.

INDEX